The *Shell Seeker*

First published in 2026
by Riverside Press, an imprint of
UniPress Books Ltd
World's End Studios
London SW10 0RJ
United Kingdom

ISBN: 978-1-917226-37-0
ISBN e-book: 978-1-917226-38-7

This book is distributed throughout the UK and Europe by
Abrams & Chronicle Books, 1 West Smithfield, London, EC1A 9JU
and 57 rue Gaston Tessier, 75166 Paris, France.
www.abramsandchronicle.co.uk
info@abramsandchronicle.co.uk

Commissioning Editor: Lucy Vallance
Art direction: Alexandre Coco
Designer: Mylène Mozas-Sauvignon
Project Manager: Ruth Patrick
Copy Editor: Beth Dymond
Picture Researcher: Alison Stevens

Printed in China
riversidepress.co.uk

1 2 3 4 5 6 7 8 9 10

Cover images: Public Domain

The *Shell Seeker*

Encounters with thirty treasures from the sea

JULI BERWALD

RIVER/IDE PRESS

Contents

Echoes of
the Ocean

Introduction

Pick up a shell at the beach; any shell at all. Does it speak to you? What is it saying? It's likely we seek shells because every one tells a story. But not just a single story. A shell is an entire library in the palm of your hand. Most of the shells you find are made by molluscs, the most diverse of all marine animals. It's estimated that there are 100,000 different species alive today, but that's probably an underestimate by half. While not all molluscs make shells (think slugs), each of the shells made by every one of these species has its own unique shape, colour, size and texture.

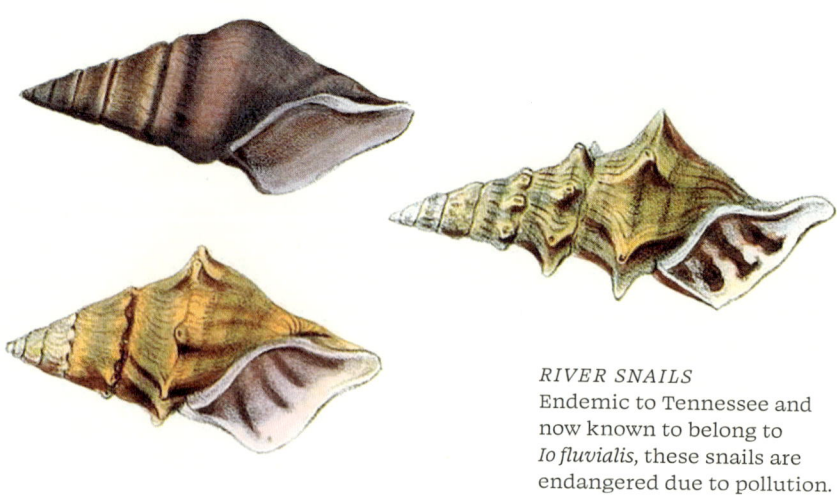

RIVER SNAILS
Endemic to Tennessee and now known to belong to *Io fluvialis*, these snails are endangered due to pollution.

Shells are the story of the eons of evolution that fashioned them into the vast variety of shapes we see in them: from an angel's wing to a child's spinning top; from an egg to a comb, a horn or a pelican's foot. The creativity of evolution honed these forms, not so that we can marvel at their beauty – although we do – but so the animal who formed them can survive.

A shell is a mollusc's protection; its defence against drying out and a structure on which to hang its muscles. It may have points and spires that make it hard for predators to gain purchase. It may be thin and angled, so it can slip through sand or bury into the mud, or it may be wide and flanged, so that it doesn't sink. Every shell shape, no matter how streamlined or intricate, is an architectural story of success.

'A shell is an entire library in the palm of your hand'

FAMILY TRIGONIIDAE
Previously known from fossils, in 1802 a living member was found in Tasmania. Today, eight species in total have been discovered.

Shell shapes

You can tell a lot about the story of the animal
that lived in a shell with a few quick observations.
The most important: is it paired or single?

A paired shell means the animal was a bivalve – one
of roughly one seventh of all molluscs. This clam,
scallop, mussel or oyster lived its life sandwiched
between two hinged shells. It could crawl around a bit,
but was largely stationary, unless it was a scallop. They
slam their shells shut with such force it creates a jet,
setting them aloft. Bivalves don't hunt. They eat using
tube-like siphons, pumping in water and filtering it
with a set of delicate gills, sustaining themselves with
a plankton buffet. Bivalves are the ocean's quiet – but
inordinately effective – cleaners.

A single shell means the mollusc was most likely a
gastropod. These snails account for three-quarters
of the mollusc species and their stories vary wildly.
A smooth, egg-shaped cowrie grew up in the tropics,
was a vegetarian as a juvenile but might have eaten
coral and sponges as an adult. If you find a hole drilled
in a shell it was likely bored by a moon snail or a whelk,
which have special mouthparts for piercing their
prey. The elegant cone snail attacks with a toxic spear.
Meanwhile, the corpulent conch grazes algae and
hops giddily over the seafloor.

A few cephalopods, relatives of the squid and octopus,
also grow a hard cover. In this book we'll meet two
of them, each with their own story of what it takes
to swim the seas in a shell.

FRESHWATER MUSSELS
Unionida is a diverse group
of bivalves, which includes
mussels that make pearls.
Fish hosts are required for
larvae survival.

Shell life stories

If you're holding a shell, turn it around in your hand. See if you can trace its story back to the beginning. Find the tiny bit at the pointy apex if it's a gastropod or the rounded umbo if it's a bivalve. That nascent nub of shell cradled the mollusc at the beginning of its life. Imagine what that was like for the animal as it metamorphosed like a butterfly from larva to an adult. For most molluscs, its world changed forever in that moment, leaving its youthful, wandering ways in the plankton and settling on the seafloor, a rock or a pier.

Look closer at the shell's changes in colours and striations. Built molecule by molecule, every shell records the chemistry of the oceans in which it lives. Like tree rings, those layers tell us about changes to our world, about hotter summers or cooler winters, about seasons with plenty to eat and seasons without. These records might require scientific tools to read, but the stories are there just the same, embedded in the atomic and crystalline structure of every shell.

Trace a path away from the shell's point of origin. Look for scars, dents or encrustations. Perhaps this shell was more than a home for the mollusc that made it. Can you spot the thin, round tube left by a feather worm, the remains of a barnacle, the stains of algae? Can you see a hole drilled by a predator? Can you see the stories of an entire community in the shell?

CASK SHELLS
Marine snails in the genus *Tonna* are named after a 'tun', a vat once used for measuring wine or honey.

Even after the animal who created it is gone, a shell's story is far from over. It may become home for another animal, like a hermit crab. If it becomes incorporated into a reef, it will also bolster coastal protection, keeping our homes safe from storms.

Otherwise, a shell may roll around on the seafloor, breaking into smaller and smaller pieces. Over time, it turns to sand and rebuilds the beach. It creates a sandy habitat for the same kinds of worms, clams and seaweeds that the animal itself once grazed upon, an endless cycle of renewal.

Or the shell might become buried in the mud. Over the millennia, it becomes a fossil – as many as 100,000 species of fossil molluscs have been identified – its calcium and carbonate replaced by silica and other minerals but maintaining the form of the shell. One day, it may be lifted high onto a mountain, where winds and rain reveal its form again.

Perhaps before the shell becomes part of a reef, returns to sand or becomes engulfed in mud, a wave lifts it into the water and deposits it on the beach. The tide peels back and leaves it exposed to the air, and that's when the shell's story crosses your path. You pick it up and consider the momentary intersection of worlds: one terrestrial and one marine; one alive and one caught up in the great geological cycle of our planet.

STRAWBERRY CLAM
Hippopus hippopus, which means 'horse foot', relies on symbiotic algae that live inside its tissues for much of its nutrition.

THE SHELL SEEKER

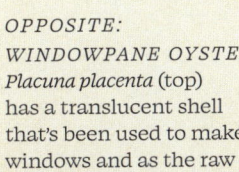

OPPOSITE:
WINDOWPANE OYSTER
Placuna placenta (top)
has a translucent shell
that's been used to make
windows and as the raw
material for glue, chalk
and varnish.

ABOVE: VENUS CLAMS
The family Veneridae
includes more than
500 species, amongst them
are most clams we eat
and these members of
the genus *Circe*.

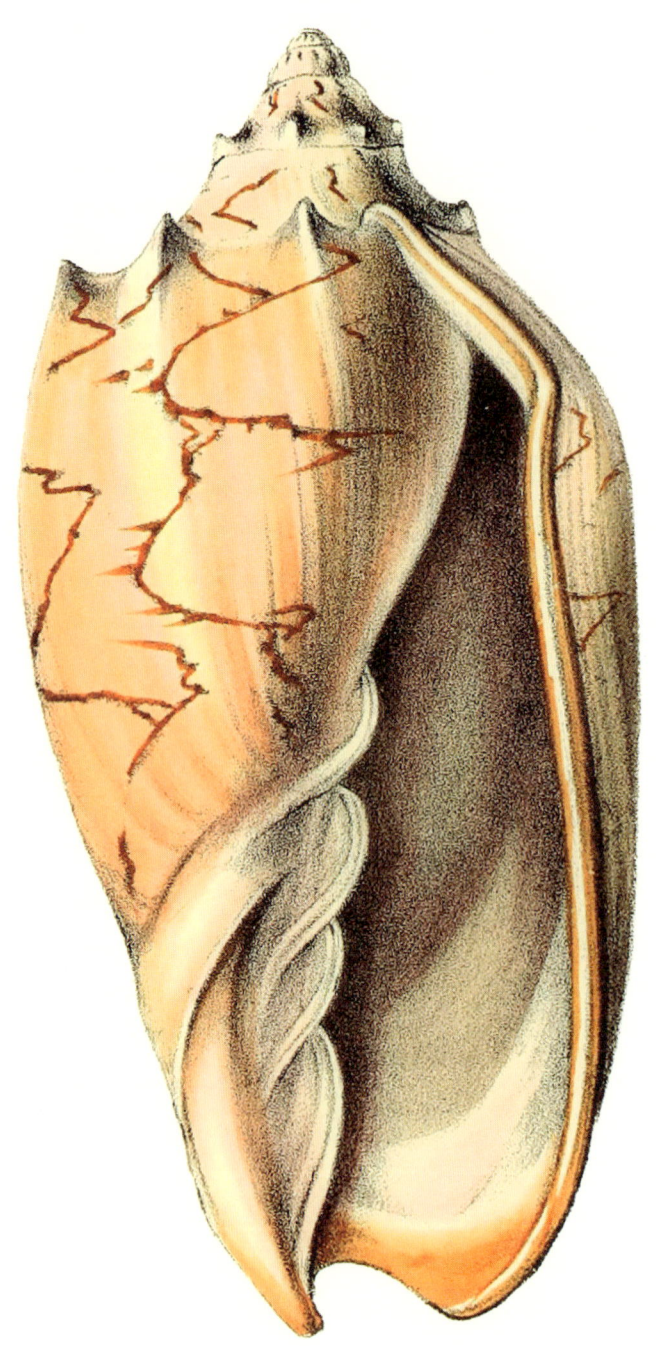

Shells speak to humans

Shells are also a story of us. The simple act of picking up a shell connects us with humans as far back as we existed, or even earlier. The first known artwork – a few etched lines on the canvas of a freshwater mussel shell – dates back 500,000 years to *Homo erectus*. We probably began eating the animals that lived inside shells back then too. The first known shell jewellery was strung together and draped across someone's neck some 100,000 years ago. The first shell instrument was filled with human breath 18,000 years ago. We traded shells for clothing, tools and food at least 2,000 years ago and the money cowrie became the common currency of the Pacific six centuries ago.

Over time, we associated shells with status, spirituality and art. Ancient people were obsessed with the blue and purple dyes produced by some molluscs, and the colour came to represent royalty. Shells were incorporated into the stories of gods, like Venus rising from the clamshell. Scallops became the metaphor of the pilgrim's journey. Shells were the muse for artists such as Georgia O'Keeffe and Salvador Dali and inspired entire movements, like Art Deco and Rococo.

In sixteenth-century Europe, wealthy collectors prized the rarest shells brought back from voyages to the Pacific. They were displayed as centrepieces of their personal menageries, curiosity cabinets that signalled social standing. Eventually, those shell collections became the foundations for our modern museums of science, our collective legacy, and our urge to pick up and hold on to the natural world.

BAT VOLUTE
Cymbiola vespertilio is a large predatory snail from the Indo-Pacific. 'Volute' means scroll, which reflects the shell's coiled, columnar shape.

It's hard not to see something of ourselves in the fascinating stories of the animals who build shells. They become a metaphor for our strengths and weaknesses, our challenges and aspirations.

Mussels, which form dense aggregations where young settle on top of the old, recognising an environment conducive to success, remind us of the importance of connection to each other. Limpets, which wear tiny imprints in the rock where they live, remind us of the comfort of home and a place to call your own. Cone snails, with their fierce venom, warn us not to be fooled by beauty, which can sometimes disguise danger. Circular moon snails, which lay their eggs in circular egg cases called collars in the sand, remind us of the reliable return of tides, seasons and life.

Pearl oysters reveal how imperfection and struggle produce the most prized of treasures. The massive abalone, with its powerful foot that holds fast to the rocks, teaches us about tenacity and strength, even as their populations dwindle. The mysterious story of sea silk, a golden fabric made from the byssus of the Mediterranean's noble pen shell, reinforces what it means to try to find balance between what we take and what we leave in the sea.

The great gift of the world's wondrous variety of shells is that no matter how many you collect, admire or discover along your way, more of their beautiful story is always waiting to be found.

AUGUR SNAILS
Named for their sharp, high-pointed spires that resemble augurs (screws), these predatory gastropods belong to the genus *Terebra*.

THE SHELL SEEKER

FANNED OUT
Though they don't live
in fresh water, roughly
250 scallop species reside
in all the world's oceans,
mostly in the Indo-Pacific.

2

The Secret World of Shells

Why Seek Shells?

The urge to pick up a shell on the shore – to feel its texture, to marvel at its architecture, to imagine what purpose it might have – runs deep in us. People seem to have sought shells for almost as long as people have been people.

Even earlier than that.

Half a million years ago, someone in Java found a clamshell on the edge of a river. They etched a zigzag on its surface to make the first known engraving. This decoration was made by our ancient cousin, *Homo erectus*.

In what would become Italy 100,000 years later, a different ancestor, the Neanderthal people, waded into the cerulean waters of the Mediterranean to seek shells. They fashioned them into knives and scrapers.

Why? Picking up a shell feels like the start of something: a discovery, an adventure, a project, a meditation. Or maybe it's just a transient encounter with nature, noticed and returned to the sea.

The best shelling happens at daybreak, when no one else has scouted the shore. In the angled light, a shell's curves cast shadows that can catch your eye. If you're on a rocky shore, shells accumulate in gullies and tide pools. A low tide can help too, when the ocean peels back its edge, revealing a bit more of itself. The wake of a storm makes for good shelling: a watery tantrum that might toss treasure your way.

If you seek a certain shell, take time to study it. Research the coasts where it's likely to be found. Find beautiful drawings like the ones in this book and photographs from different angles. Pay attention to the spikes, curves and patterns. Imagine what half the shell would look like under some seaweed. Imagine seeing it upside down in the sand.

When you're shelling, keep those patterns in the front of your mind. Look for the spots or stripes, the tulip form or the conch wing. Keep focused on the shell you are seeking. Or get distracted! You might stumble upon a shell you didn't know you were seeking. Some shellers believe that shells 'find you', and that's the best part of shelling. If you're open to whatever lies in your path, you never know what gifts will cross it.

EYE-CATCHING
Perhaps a curious beachcomber will spot a queen conch (*Aliger gigas*) on a Caribbean shore.

THE SECRET WORLD OF SHELLS

Should We Collect Shells?

You find a shell on the beach. It's lovely. It feels wonderful in your hand. But then you pause. Should you take it home? It's a question that comes with real considerations and here are some guidelines that might help with the decision.

A shell's primary role is as a home for an animal. Initially, the resident is the animal that built the shell. But even after the first occupant is gone, hermit crabs can move in. Shell surfaces are also habitats for molluscs, sea slugs, worms, sea anemones and seaweeds. If there's something living in or on the shell, it's best to return it.

As shells weather, they turn into sand. Globally, increased storms and sea level rise are eroding beaches faster. As much as half of the world's sandy shoreline could disappear by 2100. Especially where tourism is high, remember that shells are key to the beach's future. Always check local regulations about removing shells.

If you decide not to take a shell, you can still find ways to remember it. Posing a shell in front of waves, dunes or the rising sun can make for standout photos. Or try sketching shells. Start with the general form, focusing on how the scale of its parts relate to the whole. Add the whorls and ridges next, then focus on the ways that light and shadow play across the curves to create depth. With some practise, you might just create an even more meaningful memento.

SPECIOUS SNAILS
Gastropods are the most
diverse of the molluscs,
with 75,000 species. Their
varied forms reflect great
evolutionary creativity.

The Shell Builders

Most shells you'll find on a shore were built by molluscs, a massive, wildly diverse group of animals. Scientists have identified about 100,000 species, but that's only half of what's thought to exist. For comparison, just 6,600 species of mammals roam the earth. Molluscs live everywhere in the oceans, even in the most extreme conditions like hydrothermal vents, as well as lakes, rivers and on land.

The biggest mollusc class is the gastropods, or snails, about 75,000 species strong. They have a single shell, which can take on an astonishing variety of forms, from flat and domed like an abalone's, to conical like a limpet's. They can be tightly coiled or loosely spiralled; long and spiked or rounded and smooth. Some gastropods have no shells at all, like sea slugs.

The bivalves are next numerically, with between 10,000 and 20,000 species. These animals have two shells that close like a box with a hinge to protect their delicate body. They include clams, oysters, mussels and scallops.

The cephalopods, which famously include octopuses and squid, number about 800 species. While most of this class are agile swimmers and have dispensed with their shells, the nautilus has not. It bobs through the seas with a fascinating chambered shell.

The balance of the molluscs is less well known: tusk shells that don't coil at all; chitons that have eight interlocking shell plates; limpet-shaped monoplacophora that live in the deep sea; and aplacophora, a shell-less, deep-sea denizen that looks like a worm.

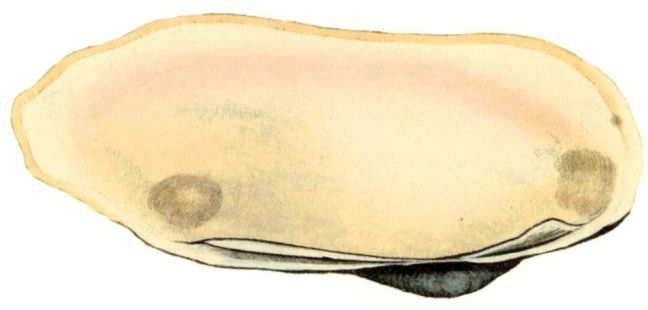

LEAVING A MARK
Bivalves' hinged shells
are held together by
adductor muscles, which
sometimes leave a scar on
the pearly nacre inside.

'Most shells you'll find on a shore were built by molluscs, a massive, wildly diverse group of animals'

Blueprint of a Shell

When you hold a shell in your hand, consider that the structure was built molecule by molecule from chemicals harvested from the seawater. The mollusc's organ responsible for shell building is called the mantle, a curtain-like tissue that surrounds the soft body of the animal.

The outermost of a shell's three layers is the periostracum. It's made from a leathery protein called conchiolin. A narrow space opens between the periostracum and the mantle where the animal secretes the minerals that crystallise to form the shell. Not just minerals but hundreds of proteins are secreted into that space, as directed by hormones. The great diversity of shell forms results from the many different ways that these molecules interact with each other.

Both inner layers of the shell are made from calcium carbonate, the same material as limestone. The animal accumulates calcium and carbonate ions from the seawater and passes them to the mantle in its blood. The middle prismatic layer is mostly made from a form of calcium carbonate called calcite, which forms rods at right angles to the outer layer of the shell.

The innermost nacreous layer is made from another form of calcium carbonate called aragonite, which grows in thin sheets. This is the layer that is iridescent in pearl oysters and abalone. Irregularities in the thin sheets break apart light waves into peacock colours. In this way, shells prove there's beauty in imperfections. Without them, the nacreous layer looks as dull as a kitchen sink.

SHELL STRUCTURES
Roughly 20,000 bivalve
species vary in shape from
boxy (top) to wedge-shaped
(middle) to the irregular
teardrop shape (below) of
the blue mussel.

'Shells prove there's
beauty in imperfections.
Without them, the
nacreous layer looks as
dull as a kitchen sink'

Bivalve shells have a few characteristic features. A ligament is located at the shell's hinge. Spring-like, it pulls the shells apart when the muscles inside relax. Inside an abandoned bivalve shell, or valve, you can see scars from those muscles, called adductors. Bivalves grow outwards from their oldest part, the umbo, in rings like a tree.

Gastropod shells, meanwhile, have given rise to a variety of scientific terms. The aperture is a fancier word for opening and its outer edge is a lip. Some gastropods seal their aperture with a door called an operculum.

The shell's top is the apex where you can find the protoconch, the oldest part. If there's a hole opposite, it is the umbilicus. Sometimes you'll see a groove along the umbilicus called the siphonal canal, where the animal sticks out a nose-like siphon. The axis runs from protoconch to umbilicus.

A gastropod's coil is called a whorl. Where two whorls connect is a suture. The distance from the apex to the biggest whorl is the spire. The outward protrusion from the biggest whorl is the shoulder. Decoration is referred to as sculpture and includes beads, ribs, nodules, tubercules or spines.

A shell is oblong if its height is bigger than its width, like a conch. In a globose or conical shell, height and width are roughly equivalent, like a periwinkle. A depressed shell has nothing to do with its mood but is one whose width is greater than its height, like a moon snail.

CONE SNAILS
Gastropods in the genus *Conus* are amongst the most diverse of all animal genera, with more than 500 species.

THE SECRET WORLD OF SHELLS

More than Molluscs

While molluscs are the most celebrated shell-makers, they are far from alone. Many marine organisms have the protection and structure that comes from growing a hard outer layer, even if it's a lot of work to build and carry it around.

The smallest shell-builders are just a single cell in size, like the foraminifera, whose single cell is similar to an amoeba. Each species builds a unique elaborate calcium carbonate shell, called a test. So many foraminifera tests have rained down on the seafloor through the millennia that they are key to understanding the earth's history. Because each species of foraminifera lives at specific temperatures, light levels, salinity and more, the presence of a particular test in sediments and fossil rocks is a little summary of past environmental conditions.

Another amoeboid shell-maker is called a radiolarian, although their outer layer is made from silica rather than calcium carbonate. Adorned with delicate spines and snowflake-like extensions, these minute glass castles also provide key information about the history of life on earth.

Diatoms, a kind of single-celled algae, build filigreed glass houses. They secrete their shells in two parts that fit together like the top and bottom of a shoebox. Coccolithophores are another kind of algae that cover themselves in intricate calcium carbonate plates. Sometimes, so many coccolithophores bloom at once that the sea looks milky white.

Millions of years of
accumulation of single-
celled, shell-bearing
coccolithophores formed
England's White Cliffs
of Dover.

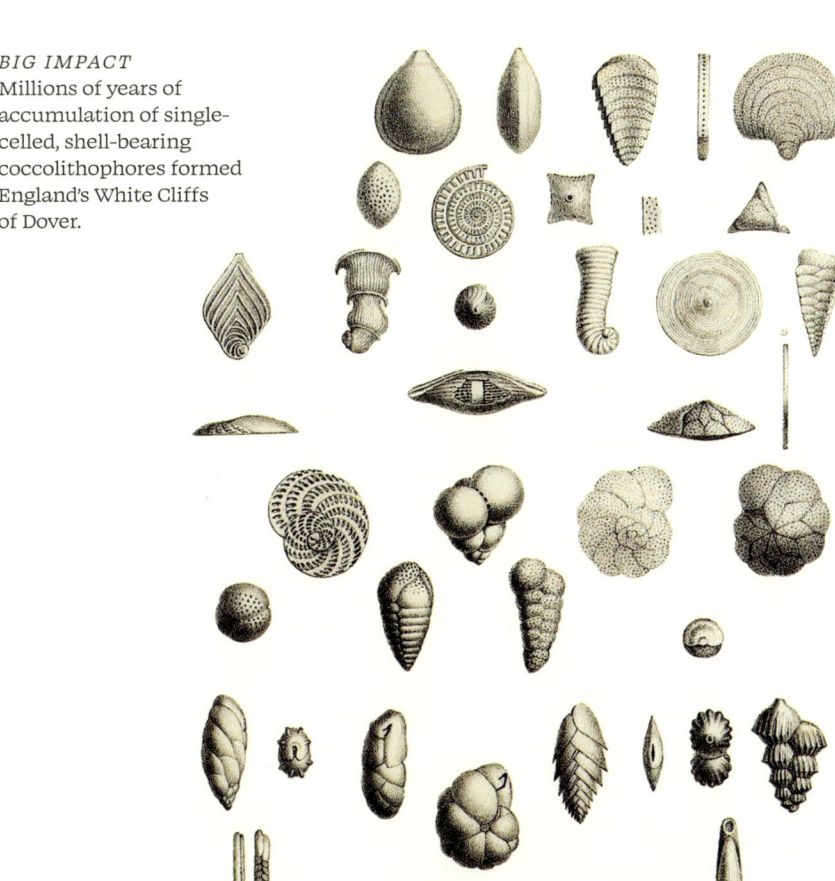

'The smallest shell-builders are just a single cell in size, like the foraminifera'

ABOVE: SPINY TESTS
The spines of the
European edible sea
urchin (*Echinus
esculentus*) fall off after the animal
dies, leaving its intricate
shell, called a test.

OPPOSITE: HOUSING
A hermit crab, *Pagurus
bernhardus,* takes up
residence inside a whelk,
upon which live barnacles
and an anemone known as
Calliactis parasitica.

Corals are iconic for their beautiful skeletons, which sometimes wash up on tropical beaches. They are aided in skeleton-building by symbiotic algae that live in their tissues. Those algae perform photosynthesis, mixing carbon dioxide with water and sunlight to form sugar. The energy in that sugar provides so much power that coral can build the great reefs of the tropics, submarine cities home to a quarter of all marine species, some 830,000.

Tube worms grow calcium carbonate shells that sometimes coil like mollusc shells. These animals have feathery feeding extensions on their heads that poke out of the top of the tube like the fronds of a tree from a trunk. When a hungry fish (or a human hand) approaches, they duck inside in the blink of an eye.

Echinoderms, whose name translates to hedgehog skin, form a stony skeleton just under a thin layer of skin. This group includes the starfish, brittle stars, sea cucumbers, sea biscuits, sand dollars, and sea urchins. The shells, or tests, of those last three are the echinoderm remains you'll likely find at the shore. Look carefully at the architecture. The holes are where the animals' many tube feet protruded.

Arthropods hold the record for diversity amongst the animals, and crustaceans are their major marine representative. They all build shells, called exoskeletons, pieces of which might wash up on a beach. The hermit crab deserves special mention for adding mollusc-derived armour to bolster its own.

The Start
of a Shell

Maybe you've stumbled over something at the beach that looks like an old telephone cord, the vent to a clothes dryer, a plastic collar or a broken sconce, but upon closer inspection it's not anything you'd find at a hardware store. Maybe it crumbles at the touch. Maybe if you peer closely, you see pockets filled with seawater and – if you're lucky – baby molluscs.

Like butterflies, molluscs start their lives as larvae that go through huge changes, but many molluscs do butterflies one better and metamorphise not once but twice. (Still, the record holders are crustaceans, which can go through over a dozen.)

A mollusc's first larval stage is called a trochophore, which means wheel-bearer in Greek. The top of these tiny creatures' heads is a circular swirl of cilia. This beats in a wave that looks like a spinning wheel. Trochophores are part of the plankton, and that spinning wheel keeps them afloat.

In the second larval stage, the veliger, the animal develops a vellum, two veil-like lobes, both fringed in cilia. Now the larva has two wheels for swimming in the plankton.

Veligers also develop a foot that can explore the seafloor for a place that feels like home. When the time is right, the larva leaves the open sea and settles down.

But some species of molluscs don't risk releasing their offspring into the wilds of the ocean for their formative weeks. Instead, these crafty mollusc mothers use saliva, mucus and sometimes sand to build egg cases (such as those of whelks, opposite, and conchs, below) where their babies pass their larval life. These offspring hatch directly into the sea, ready to meet the world shell on.

'Like butterflies, molluscs start their lives as larvae that go through huge changes'

Early Conchologists

In Western texts, discussion of molluscs started during the time of Aristotle, who observed: 'Cockles and clams and razor-clams and scallops grow spontaneously in sandy places. The pen shell grows straight up from its tuft of anchoring fibres . . . common sorts, such as the limpet and the nerites . . . grow with great rapidity.'

That last mollusc is a small, striking, black-and-white gastropod whose namesake is the sea-god Nerites. In one version of his tale, Nerites was Aphrodite's lover, who refused to accompany her to Mount Olympus. In another, he was Poseidon's lover, which angered Helios, god of the sun. In both, the poor deity was transformed into a snail as punishment.

Two centuries later, Pliny the Elder wrote raucously of sea creatures such as merpeople and sea-elephants. He also had some misguided thoughts about oysters and starfish having 'no sensation whatsoever . . . the same nature as vegetables'. He did, however, know about raising snails and oysters in ponds, 'fattening them with new wine boiled down', which might have made for a twist on escargot.

Cicero, in *De Oratore*, wrote that his father 'used to gather shells and pebbles at Caieta and Laurentum'. In the same passage, he wrote that shell-collecting provides serenity amidst political turmoil, which holds as true today.

It wasn't until 1691 that Filippo Buonanni published the first book on molluscs in Rome. Rife with delightful anatomical mistakes, it nonetheless correctly divides the mollusc phylum into bivalves, snails and everything else.

DELIGHTFUL DRAWINGS
Illustrations from the
first book on shells,
enchantingly titled *For the
Delight of the Eyes and the
Mind in Observing Snails.*

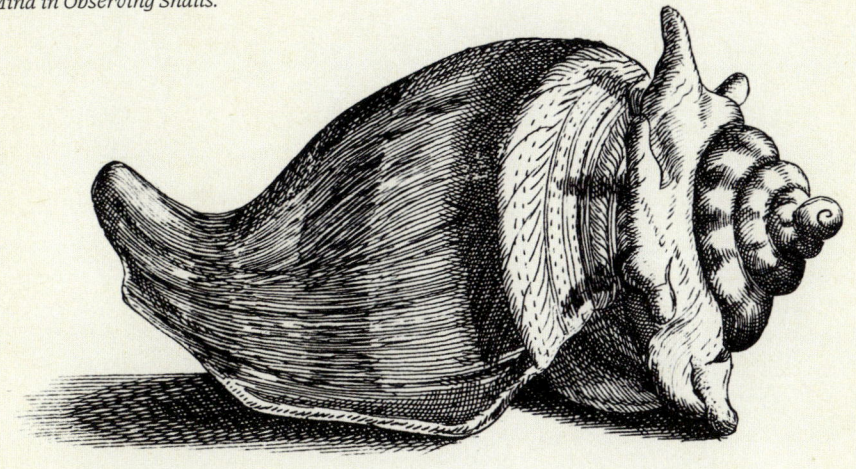

Conchylomania

As the Dutch East India Company, established in 1602, roamed the seas from the tip of Africa to the eastern Pacific in the search for treasures, sailors were amazed at the great variety of shells they encountered. They combed beaches and engaged locals to dive into the sea and bring back the most colourful and ornamental shells. These shells returned to Europe and were sold from the docks.

Shells were all the rage. It became a status and fashion statement to arrange the shells in special displays, called *Kunstkammers*, or curiosity cabinets to show off to guests. Wealthy collectors posed with shells for portraits. The highly ornamental Rococo style incorporated shells on furniture and architecture. Much like the tulip craze that blossomed in the Netherlands a few decades earlier, conchylomania engulfed Europe.

One of the most prolific shell collectors was Albertus Seba, a pharmacist. As his treasury grew, he commissioned a book that spanned four volumes, the shells artfully arranged in decorative plates. When Russia's Peter the Great came to visit Amsterdam, Seba sold him seventy-two drawers full of his compendium, which became a central exhibit at Russia's first museum, Kunstkamera, in St. Petersburg.

Conchylomania leaves two key lessons for us today: the mollusc menageries were stolen objects, taken during a time of unfettered colonisation, and these shells represent awe and understanding of the richness of our planet's marine life.

**PHARMACIST'S
TREASURE**
In 1734, Albertus Seba
published his *Thesaurus*
of natural curiosities,
including pages of
artfully arranged
cowries like these.

Shelves of Shells

Today, you can see hundreds of millions of mollusc shells, not in the sea or on the shore, but in displays, shelves and drawers. In the United States and Canada, an estimated eighty-six natural history collections house more than 100 million specimens, of which only about three-quarters have been catalogued. In Europe, that number is estimated at 30 million specimens in hundreds of museums and collections of various sizes.

The Smithsonian National Museum of Natural History houses the most mollusc shells, with more than 15 million specimens. Two historic surveys formed the foundation of this vast collection and of malacology: the US Exploring Expedition (1838–42), which confirmed the existence of the Antarctic continent, and the Albatross Voyages (1883–1921), which explored the marine biodiversity of the Americas and the Philippines.

London's Natural History Museum is the world's second largest and houses 8 million shells, many of which came from curiosity cabinets throughout Europe. Amongst the shells at the Natural History Museum are a special subset collected by Joseph Banks, the scientist who accompanied Captain Cook on his voyages across the oceans. Banks had a penchant for picking up shells; all his finds are just the right size to slip inside a pocket.

A huge effort is underway to put shell collections online. About half have undergone some form of digitisation. As this process continues, shells will not only exist on shores and shelves, but anywhere anyone with curiosity wants them to be.

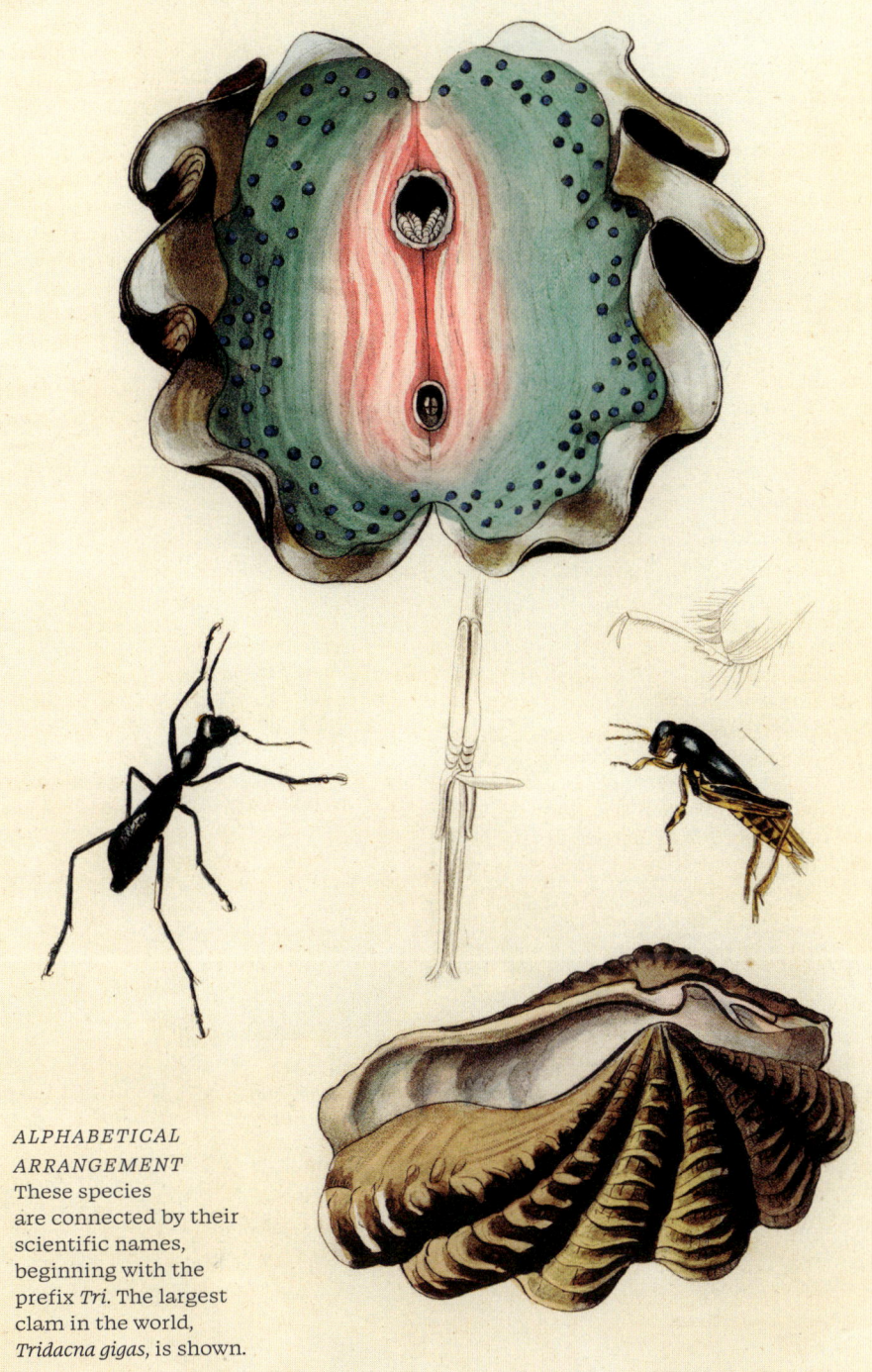

ALPHABETICAL ARRANGEMENT These species are connected by their scientific names, beginning with the prefix *Tri*. The largest clam in the world, *Tridacna gigas*, is shown.

THE SECRET WORLD OF SHELLS

Hinged Shells

The word Bivalvia comes from a combination of the Latin words *bi,* meaning two, and *valva,* meaning leaves or flaps of a hinged door. It refers to the two hinged shells that are characteristic of this class of mussels, oysters, clams and scallops.

The group has gone through some name changes over the eons. They were once called Lamellibranchia, which roughly translates to 'thin-layered gills' because these hinged molluscs both breathe and eat by pumping water through very fine sheets of tissue that filter food into their stomach and absorb oxygen into their blood. Bivalves move the water across these gills using two siphons: one for inhaling and one for exhaling water.

The class has also gone by the moniker Pelecypoda, which had its roots in Greek and means axe-footed. Most bivalves can't swim (one key exception being scallops) and many of them dig into the sand or mud. They clear the way with a muscular part of their body called a foot.

Bivalves are an extremely successful group of animals. Their shells populate the fossil record for half a billion years. Today, between 10,000 and 20,000 species are known to exist. Over 86 percent of those live in the ocean and the rest in fresh water. Notable is the large family of freshwater mussels, Unionidae, which has a whopping 700 species. With so much diversity, there's a wide array of bivalve shapes and sizes. The micro-clam *Condylonucula maya* grows to a length of about 500 micrometers, while the massive giant clam, *Tridacna gigas,* clocks in at nearly 1.3 m (4 ft).

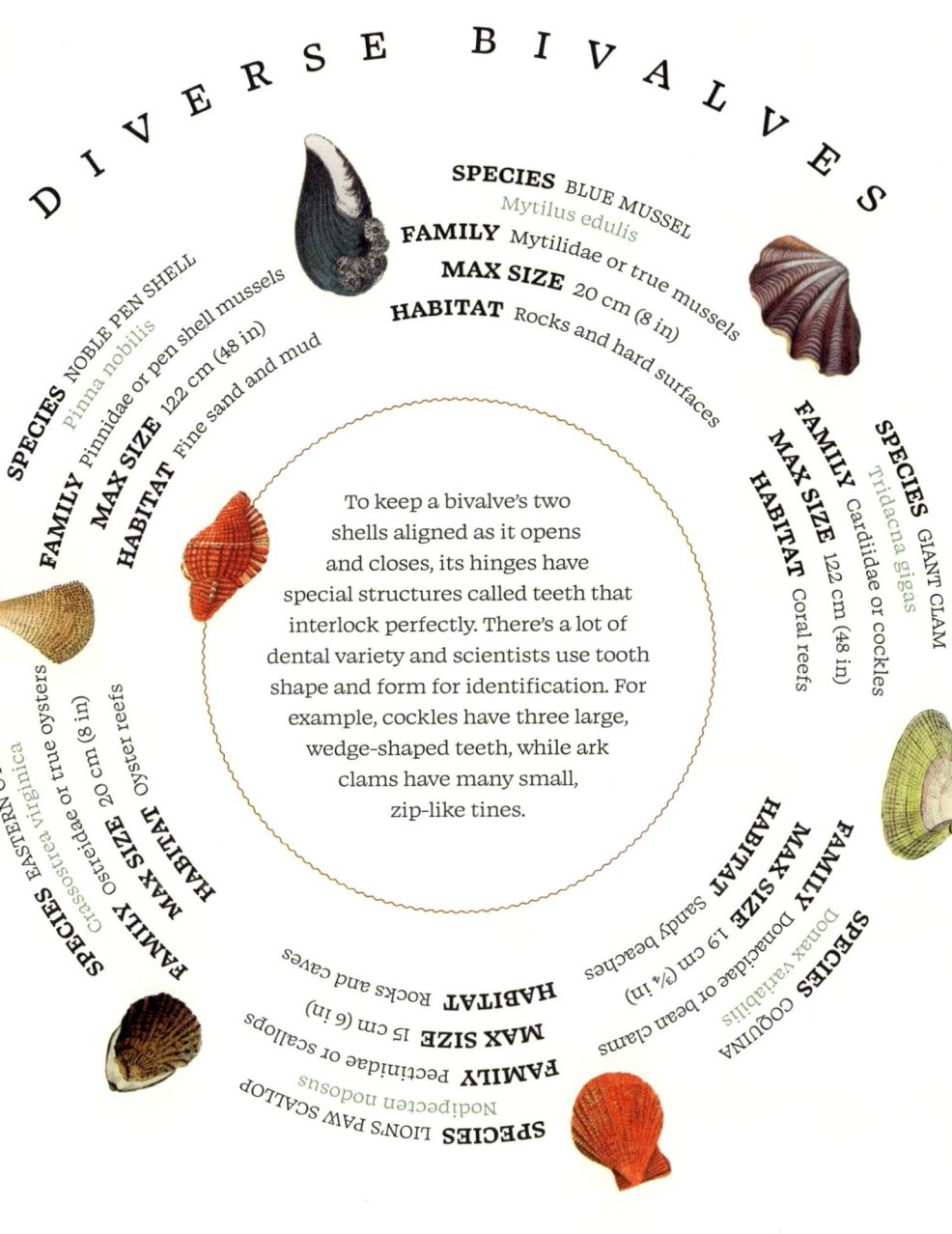

DIVERSE BIVALVES

SPECIES BLUE MUSSEL
Mytilus edulis
FAMILY Mytilidae or true mussels
MAX SIZE 20 cm (8 in)
HABITAT Rocks and hard surfaces

SPECIES NOBLE PEN SHELL
Pinna nobilis
FAMILY Pinnidae or pen shell mussels
MAX SIZE 122 cm (48 in)
HABITAT Fine sand and mud

SPECIES GIANT CLAM
Tridacna gigas
FAMILY Cardiidae or cockles
MAX SIZE 122 cm (48 in)
HABITAT Coral reefs

SPECIES EASTERN OYSTER
Crassostrea virginica
FAMILY Ostreidae or true oysters
MAX SIZE 20 cm (8 in)
HABITAT Oyster reefs

SPECIES COQUINA
Donax variabilis
FAMILY Donacidae or bean clams
MAX SIZE 19 cm (¾ in)
HABITAT Sandy beaches

SPECIES LION'S PAW SCALLOP
Nodipecten nodosus
FAMILY Pectinidae or scallops
MAX SIZE 15 cm (6 in)
HABITAT Rocks and caves

To keep a bivalve's two shells aligned as it opens and closes, its hinges have special structures called teeth that interlock perfectly. There's a lot of dental variety and scientists use tooth shape and form for identification. For example, cockles have three large, wedge-shaped teeth, while ark clams have many small, zip-like tines.

The Scallop's Way

The ancient pilgrimage of the Camino de Santiago follows a set of trails that lead to the Cathedral of St. James in Galicia, in Northwest Spain. You can reach the network from anywhere in Europe, but on the Iberian Peninsula the trails form a fan from western Portugal to northern Spain and converge on Santiago de Compostela. The pattern is reminiscent of the rays on a scallop, all converging at the umbo, the oldest point on the shell.

Two legends explain the association between Saint James and the scallop. One says that after he was killed in the Galilee, his body was returned to Spain but a terrible storm destroyed the ship. Miraculously, the remains washed ashore covered in scallop shells. Another says that his remains were returned in a ship with no crew. A wedding was taking place as the ghostly ship bearing Saint James's remains sailed past. The groom's horse was spooked and ran into the ocean. When the horse and rider emerged they were safe but covered in scallops.

In the past, some pilgrims would collect their scallop at the end of their walk – proof they reached the ocean and completed the pilgrimage. Today, they often collect their shell at a shop along the way to hang on their backpacks or around their necks. Seeing these icons, other pilgrims contemplate the powerful spiritual metaphor: there are many ways to travel; many journeys to take. Each of us must find our own way to get where we need to go.

JET SET
Unlike most bivalves, scallops are far from sessile. They can jet around the seafloor by snapping their shells together.

Sea Silk

In the second century CE, a Chinese writer known
as Yu Huan penned a fascinating note about the people
of the Mediterranean: 'They weave fine cloth, saying
that they utilise for this purpose the down of the water-
sheep; this product is termed "cloth from the west of the
sea" (*hai si pu*).'

This 'water-sheep' is the bivalve *Penna nobilis*, the largest
pen shell in the Mediterranean. Its 'wool' is the thin and
strong threads it secretes, called byssus, which help hold
it steady in the muddy bottom where it lives. When woven
into a thread, the byssus is known as sea silk. Treasured for
its lightness, warmth and stunning golden colour, Yu Huan
confirms this precious textile was traded as far as China
almost two millennia ago.

Today, the noble pen shell is endangered because
of overfishing, pollution and disease. Amongst the last
remaining sea silk seamstresses is Chiara Vigo, who
lives on the island of Sardinia. She has special permission
to collect noble pen byssus, but only that which will not
harm the animal, and the Italian Coast Guard accompanies
her on collecting trips. It takes Vigo months to collect and
spin byssus into sea silk. The process includes bathing
the spun threads in fifteen types of seaweed.

For Vigo, working with sea silk is both a privilege and
a responsibility. She observes a pact by which her work
can neither be bought or sold; it can only be given
and received as a gift from the sea.

ANCIENT THREADS
The oldest surviving
sea silk is a fourteenth-
century cap found in
an archaeological site's
waste pit in Paris.

THE SECRET WORLD OF SHELLS

Who's Got a Button?

If you dig through a rack of vintage suits, you might come across a button that has a particular lustre and shine, one that has a slight curve and doesn't look factory-made. It's probably made from a shell.

Up until the early 1900s, people's clothing was held together with fasteners made from natural materials: wood, bone and horn. But if you wanted to elevate the clothes you owned, your buttons would be made from shells. Mother-of-pearl, its iridescence born of the nacre layer inside a mollusc, was most highly prized.

Using a tube-like drill, button-makers in New England punched circular holes in mollusc shells: black abalone (*Haliotis cracherodii*) from the California coast, pearl oyster (*Pinctada maxima*) and cone top shell (*Tectus conus*) from the South Pacific, and toothed top shell (*Tectus dentatus*) from the Indian Ocean.

The most important were freshwater yellow sandshell mussels (*Lampsilis teres*) from the Mississippi River, which were bigger, flatter and easier to obtain than their marine counterparts. A massive button industry arose on the banks of the Mississippi, which employed half the population from Minnesota to Iowa and produced 37 percent of the world's buttons in 1905: a whopping 1.5 billion.

Cheaper, durable plastic and the psychedelic styles of the 1960s led to the rise of big, colourful buttons that couldn't be made from shells, and the end of the era of the bivalve button.

BUTTON BUSINESS
Muscatine, Iowa, the
Pearl Button Capital of
the World, has a museum
celebrating pearl buttons
from shells such as these.

A Grotto of Gastropods

In 1835, the story goes, a boy and his father – or perhaps some workmen – were digging a pond in a residential back garden in the coastal town of Margate, Kent. They uncovered a hole in the earth. Excavating deeper, they saw it was a tunnel. Lowering themselves into the subterranean passage, the light of their torches revealed a vast grotto decorated in mosaics of millions of molluscs.

The winding passageway of the Shell Grotto is about 2.5 m (8 ft) high and 18 m (60 ft) long, ending in a square, shrine-like room. A domed ceiling is made from concentric rings of shells. The patterns – all manner of swirls, circles, flowers and hearts – cover every square inch of the cave's walls and ceilings. Most of the shells are local mussels, scallops, oysters, limpets, slipper shells and whelks, although the flat winkle (*Littorina obtusata* or *Littorina fabalis*) is rarely found in Margate and might have been brought from elsewhere.

Other shell grottos exist. In the 1600s, King James I had one built in Whitehall Palace and the Duke of Bedford built one at Woburn Abbey. By the end of the century, shell grottos were popular features of country houses, cool sanctuaries that evoked the sea.

What makes Margate's Shell Grotto so mysterious is that there's no record of who built it or why. No one knows if it was a place of worship, of secret meetings or simply of retreat from the world. In that uncertainty, it becomes a place of enduring wonder.

SUNRAY SHELLS
These clams belong to
various genera, including
Gari (sunset shells),
Tellina (tellins), *Ervilia,*
Scrobicularia, Donax
(bean or wedge shells),
and *Mactra.*

Shells with Spikes

From bivalves to gastropods, molluscs grow shells with ridges, varices, spines, combs and blades. These remarkable sculptures are gorgeous to look at, and shells with extensions are more sought after by collectors. But such ostentation also provides advantages to the animals. Sharp needles deter predators. Thick ridges strengthen the shell. Broad blades stabilise the animal as it crawls and help to prevent it from sinking into the mud.

The trick to forming mollusc embellishments comes from the interaction of the mantle, which is the tissue that surrounds the mollusc, and the location where the new shell is being secreted but isn't yet calcified, called the generative zone. If the mollusc's body doesn't grow at the exact same rate as its shell, the generative zone will deform and solidify.

Spines are the most common extension. They happen when the mollusc's mantle has a growth spurt. To fit itself to the shell, the generative zone has to buckle, like folding a piece of cloth into a pleat. Then it hardens that way. As the pleat is reinforced with new layers of shell, it grows into a spine. Faster growth leads to longer, narrower extensions.

Scientists speculate that the cues for where to place the shell's adornments come from the mantle sensing the distance from the previous ones. In the Venus comb murex, some tritons, and helmet snails, they are at 120 degrees from each other, but in the maple leaf triton (*Gyrineum perca*) they are 180 degrees. Still others are mystifyingly random.

SPINY SHELLS

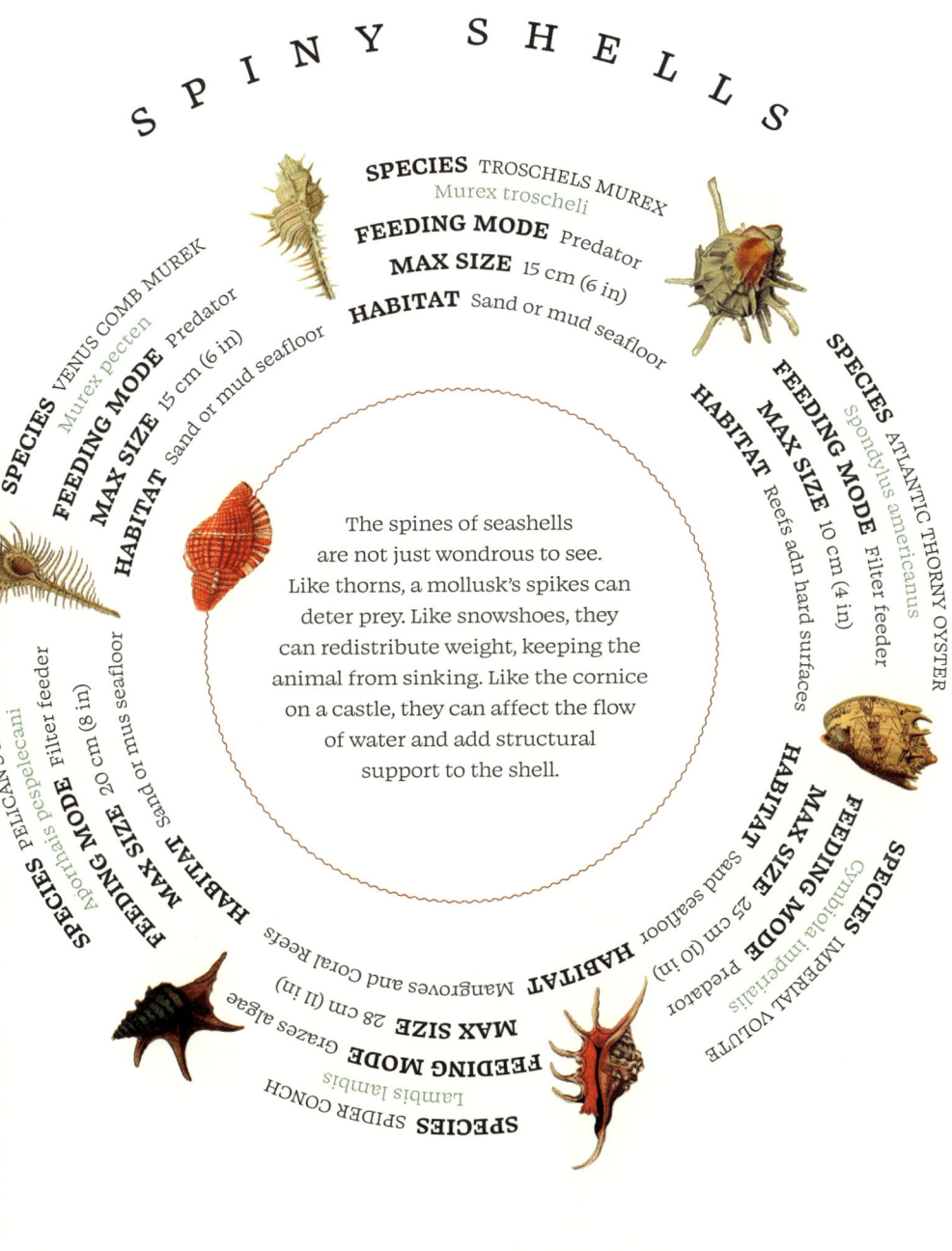

SPECIES TROSCHELS MUREX
Murex troscheli
FEEDING MODE Predator
MAX SIZE 15 cm (6 in)
HABITAT Sand or mud seafloor

SPECIES VENUS COMB MUREK
Murex pecten
FEEDING MODE Predator
MAX SIZE 15 cm (6 in)
HABITAT Sand or mud seafloor

SPECIES ATLANTIC THORNY OYSTER
Spondylus americanus
FEEDING MODE Filter feeder
MAX SIZE 10 cm (4 in)
HABITAT Reefs adn hard surfaces

The spines of seashells are not just wondrous to see. Like thorns, a mollusk's spikes can deter prey. Like snowshoes, they can redistribute weight, keeping the animal from sinking. Like the cornice on a castle, they can affect the flow of water and add structural support to the shell.

SPECIES PELICAN'S FOOT
Aporrhais pespelecani
FEEDING MODE Filter feeder
MAX SIZE 20 cm (8 in)
HABITAT Sand or mus seafloor

SPECIES IMPERIAL VOLUTE
Cymbiola imperialis
FEEDING MODE Predator
MAX SIZE 25 cm (10 in)
HABITAT Sand seafloor

SPECIES SPIDER CONCH
Lambis lambis
FEEDING MODE Grazes algae
MAX SIZE 28 cm (11 in)
HABITAT Mangroves and coral reefs

The Sound of the Sea

According to anthropologists, no society exists without song; no ritual or celebration occurs without accompanying sound. In Oceania, New Zealand, Europe, India, Japan, Indochina, the Caribbean and beyond, people blow through, rattle or clang shells together to connect, celebrate and share human experiences.

The first shell known to be transformed into an instrument was a conch (*Charonia lampas*) found in a cave in the foothills of the Pyrenees in France. Carbon dating revealed the inhabitants lived in the cave about 18,000 years ago. The mollusc was from the North Atlantic, so someone must have moved it a long distance.

The shell was discovered in 1931 but ignored for 80 years until anthropologists noticed some intentional modifications. The apex was removed, creating a hole, and similar holes were drilled in the internal whorls near the central spiral. They realised you could fit a hollow bone inside the top of the shell, creating a mouthpiece that could be held in place by the remains of a kind of waxy resin that was present. The shell lip was smoothed to make it comfortable to hold. Dots of red pigment and etchings were visible, indicating ancient decoration.

The anthropologists entrusted a talented horn player to test the instrument, bringing into being the millennial-old sounds of the shell. The horn released three notes, corresponding to a C, C sharp and D – or what we understand as half-note steps – each low and sonorous note a reverberation through time.

TRIDENT TRUMPET
Charonia lampas is a
predatory gastropod also
known as the pink lady,
which lives in the Atlantic
and Indian oceans.

'No
society
exists
without
song'

The Radical Radula

Molluscs have mouths, but rather than teeth and a tongue, all except the bivalves have a structure that's a combination of both, and more. This toothy tongue is called a radula, meaning 'little scraper' in Latin.

In gastropods, the radula is long – even as long as the animal itself – and usually covered in small teeth. These teeth overlap with each other and form rows that look like the treads on a car tyre. The radula wraps around a hard, rounded piece of cartilage, similar to a bike chain around a gear. The snail can extend the cartilage like sticking out its tongue. This forces the teeth on the radula to stand on end. Muscles then slide the radula over the cartilage, scooping food towards the digestive system. This abrasive action continually wears down the radula's teeth, so the snail has to make new ones. An average snail radula has about 100,000 teeth, so it's no trifling task.

What makes the radula amazing is that it's so modifiable, accommodating the vast array of feeding needs that support the great biodiversity of the molluscs. If a snail scrubs algae, its radula will have many tiny, pointed teeth. If it prises small worms and barnacles from rocks, many blunt blades are better. If it's a predator, the teeth are armed with toxins that first dissolve its prey's shell and then dissolve the meat inside. Cone snails have a radula with a single venomous tooth that's like a spear. Squid and octopus radulae are modified for cutting up prey.

RUTHLESS RADULA
A cone snail's radula is incorporated into a complex venom apparatus, hence the saying: 'If it's a cone, leave it alone.'

THE SECRET WORLD OF SHELLS

Left- and Right-handed Snails

Hold a snail shell in your hand with the apex pointed up and the aperture facing you. Odds are the opening will be on the right side. More than 90 percent of gastropod species are built this way. They are called right-handed or dextral.

If you happen to be holding a lightning whelk (*Sinistrofulgur perversum*) from the southeastern US or a land snail in the genus *Diplommatina* from southern Asia, the aperture will be on the left, making it left-handed or sinistral.

In some species, the population is predominately right-handed but a low proportion is left-handed. One example is the escargot snail, *Helix pomatia*. Because of their rarity, left-handed shells are prized by collectors.

Such left/right asymmetry might remind you of humans. Like the molluscs, about 10 percent of us are left-handed and no one knows why. Some propose left-handedness adds creativity to the population because the brain of a left-hander is organised slightly differently from a right-hander.

Scientists also wonder why left-handed snails persist in low percentages. Left-handed snails might confuse predators who are used to attacking right-handed prey or it might be a source of variation, the fuel for new species to arise.

What scientists studying humans and molluscs do know is that a low level of left-handedness must have some advantage because it keeps sticking around. Left-handedness has arisen nineteen times in different groups of gastropods. In humans, the 10 percent number holds across all continents and all cultures.

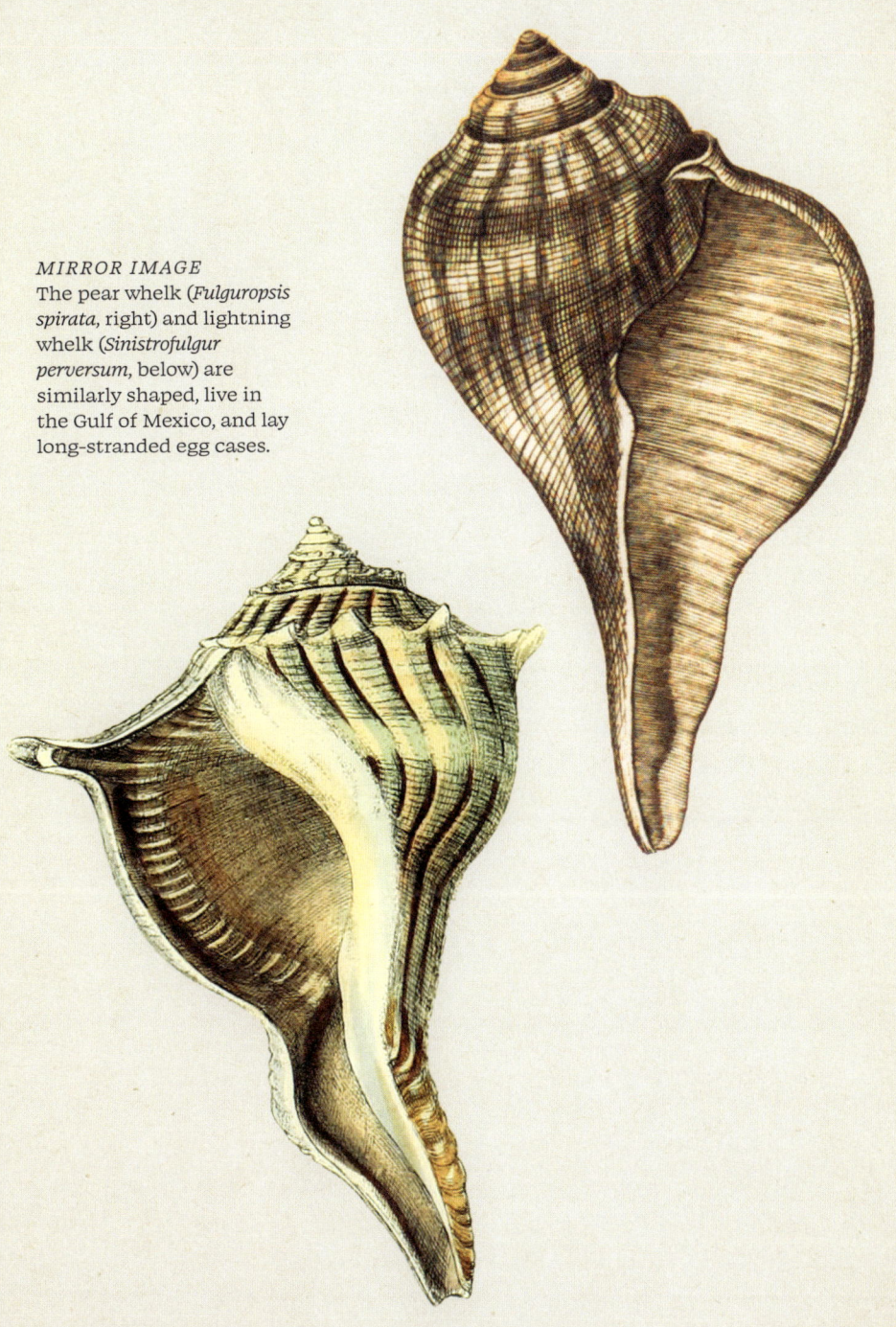

MIRROR IMAGE
The pear whelk (*Fulguropsis spirata*, right) and lightning whelk (*Sinistrofulgur perversum*, below) are similarly shaped, live in the Gulf of Mexico, and lay long-stranded egg cases.

Molluscs in the Extreme

In 1977, the scientific submersible *Alvin* was lowered 2.5 km (1½ mi) to the seafloor in the Pacific Ocean. Three men sat cramped in the small space as they descended into the deep, cold water. When they arrived at their target, the water suddenly warmed from near freezing to 8°C (46°F). It shimmered up from the seafloor, turning cloudy blue as minerals in the warm water formed compounds with those in the surrounding seawater. This was the discovery of the first hydrothermal vent.

What astonished the deep-sea-faring men was that like an oasis on a barren ocean floor, lush life grew around the vent, especially molluscs. Amongst strange orange puffballs and red-tipped worms, they saw dense fields of foot-long white clams and brown mussels.

'Like an oasis on a barren ocean floor, lush life grew around the vent, especially molluscs'

'Today, we've discovered hundreds of vents that support animals, fuelled by the chemistry of the seawater'

Today, we've discovered hundreds of hydrothermal vents dotting the deep sea that support a multitude of unique animal communities, fuelled not by the sun but by the chemistry of the seawater. Molluscs, of which at least 184 vent species exist, dominate these extreme habitats. New species are constantly being discovered, like the scaly-foot gastropod (*Chrysomallon squamiferum*) which has iron armour in its foot. Many animals are highly endemic, only living at one or two vents. Rarely is a vent home to more than ten mollusc species. Scientists fear that proposed deep-sea mining could threaten the existence of these incredible animals before we've even had a chance to know who they are.

The Colour Purple

According to myth, the god Hercules was walking on the beach with his dog when the pet seized upon a snail. The pooch bit down and his mouth was stained in an arresting purple. A nymph, hovering nearby, was entranced by the colour. She demanded that Hercules create a gown for her with the dye, thus bringing the colour purple into existence.

In fact, people have been using gastropods to make purple dye as far back as the eighteenth century BCE. Archaeologists discovered the pigment on pottery at ancient sites in Crete. The purple colour's source is a family of predatory murex gastropods known to make pigments from blue to red as well, all of which might have been called purple in ancient times. A gland under the snail's mantle secretes a pigmented fluid to sedate its prey and to swath their eggs in an antimicrobial cover.

The people of Tyre, in what was Phoenicia (now Lebanon), made the snail-rendered dye world famous as Tryian purple beginning around 1200 BCE. Rather than fade with time, it was said to brighten with wear. Twelve thousand snails (mostly *Murex brandaris* in Tyre, though other species were used elsewhere) were required to make enough dye to trim the edge of one garment. The process was so arduous that the dye sold for as much as silver and was kept in state treasuries. Purple became the colour of royalty and remains so today.

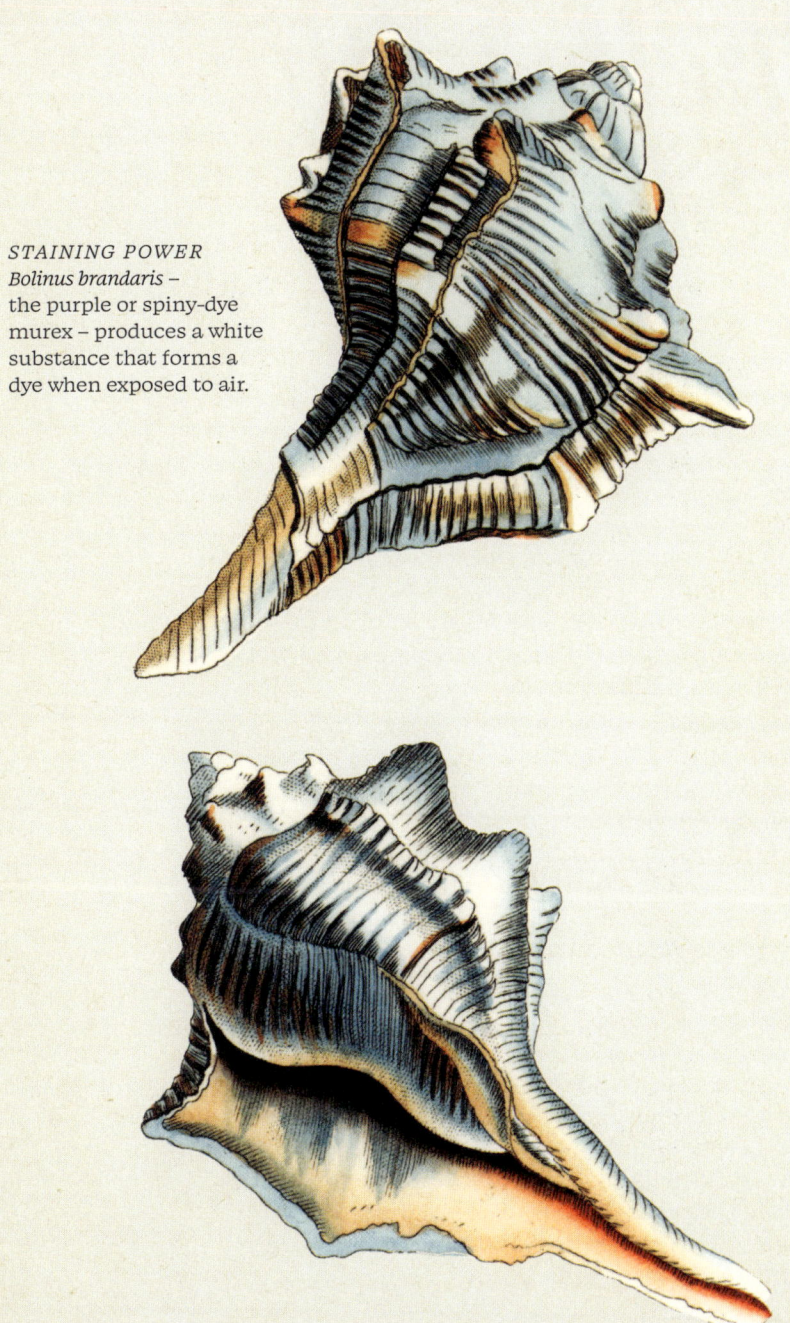

STAINING POWER
Bolinus brandaris –
the purple or spiny-dye
murex – produces a white
substance that forms a
dye when exposed to air.

Shells with Shine

Cowries belong to the family Cypraeidae. This refers to the island of Cyprus, the birthplace of Aphrodite, the goddess of love and beauty. Indeed, these shells are sought after for their exquisiteness. They have also been connected to reproduction and fertility, either because of their egg-like shape or their similarity to a woman's pregnant belly. In Japan, women hold cowries during childbirth and in Polynesia they are thought to assure fertility. Cowries are also associated with divination and were amongst the first forms of money in the world.

One reason for cowries' attractiveness is that their shells remain shiny throughout the animal's adult life. That's because the mantle, the part of the gastropod responsible for creating the shell, can extend up out of the zip-toothed aperture in the bottom and surround its entire surface. As it does so, the mantle cleans the shell of debris or the advances of encrusting organisms and mends any damage. During the process, the mantle also polishes the shell to its lustrous shine.

More than 270 species of cowries live near coral and rocky reefs in tropical waters in the Indian and Pacific oceans, though some also live in the Atlantic and Mediterranean. They range in size from the large Atlantic deer cowrie, which reaches 20 cm (8 in), to the smallest, which are just 6 mm (¼ in). Cowrie shells are adorned with some of the most interesting coloration, from stripes or dots to smudges of all hues. These patterns aid in camouflage on the reef and our admiration of their beauty.

SPECIES MONEY COWRIE
Monetaria moneta
PATTERN Sometimes pale stripes
MAX SIZE 3 cm (1¼ in)
HABITAT Rocky shoreline

SPECIES TIGER COWRIE
Murex pecten
PATTERN Brown dots
MAX SIZE 15 cm (6 in)
HABITAT Coral reefs

SPECIES CHOCOLATE BANDED COWRIE
Talparia talpa
PATTERN Brown bands
MAX SIZE 2.3 cm (⅞ in)
HABITAT Coral reefs

Cowries mostly dwell
near coral reefs in tropical seas,
where they emerge at night to graze
algae. But a few prefer cooler waters.
The European cowrie and its cousin the
Arctic cowrie range from the Mediterranean up to Norway. The Atlantic
deer cowrie can be found as far
north as South Carolina.

SPECIES ATLANTIC DEER COWRIE
Macrocypraea cervus
PATTERN White dots
MAX SIZE 19 cm (7½ in)
HABITAT Coral reefs

SPECIES CHESTNUT COWRIE
Neobernaya spadicea
PATTERN Uniform brown
MAX SIZE 6.5 cm (2½ in)
HABITAT Kelp beds

SPECIES LITTLE DEER COWRIE
Macrocypraea cervinetta
PATTERN White dots
MAX SIZE 11cm (4⅜ in)
HABITAT Coral reefs

The Feminine Shell

Across cultures and centuries, shells – especially cowries and scallops – have been potent symbols of femininity. Their curved, enclosed forms resemble female genitalia, linking them to fertility, sexuality and the generative power of women. Anthropologists suggest shells' symbolism also arises from their function: vessels that hold and protect life, much like a womb.

In Western cultures, this association is immortalised in Sandro Botticelli's *Birth of Venus*. The goddess of love and beauty emerges from an open scallop to represent that she is born, like a pearl, from the sea.

Amongst the Yoruba of West Africa, the goddess Yemoja is recognised as mother of all orishas, or divine spirits. She rules over rivers and seas and protects women. When her waters broke, myth says they formed the rivers and oceans. Cowrie shells, used in female puberty rites and fertility ceremonies to invoke her blessing, symbolise her power.

In Tonga, the sea goddess Hina is adorned with coral and shells. Like Venus and Yemoja, she embodies fertility, birth and water's generative force. She calms storms, governs the tides and guards the ocean's biodiversity. Recognising her as the provider and protector of marine life, fisherpeople ask her blessing and to share in the bounty she protects.

Around the world, shells are viewed as sacred symbols of the feminine divine: vessels of life, protectors of fertility and emblems of the sea's abundance. They reflect a shared human understanding: that water, birth and the feminine are deeply intertwined.

Botticelli could have been inspired by the great scallop, *Pecten maximus,* from the northeast Atlantic.

'Anthropologists suggest shells' symbolism also arises from their function: vessels that hold and protect life, much like a womb'

How Many Clams for That?

Because they are easy to hold, easy to hand over to other people and only found in limited locations, shells rose to exceptional importance in ancient economies around the world. The original queen of shell finance was Sultana Rehendhi Khadijah, who ruled the Maldives for three decades in the fourteenth century, amongst the few women to ever rule the island nation in its long history. Sultana Khadijah was an impressive leader, wrestling control of her archipelago from men three times by having them assassinated: first her brother and then both of her husbands.

The Maldives are a chain of twenty-six coral atolls in the Indian Ocean, home to a flat, white cowrie with a domed top and serrated slit that has a similar shape and heft as a coin. The prolific animal namer, Carl Linnaeus, gave it the scientific name *Cypraea moneta* in the 1600s. It is now known as *Monetaria moneta*, or the money cowrie.

Amongst Sultana Khadijah's greatest accomplishments was developing the original global finance system based on the money cowrie. Because the gastropod grows to a uniform size and can be weighed instead of counted, the shell was an ideal form of money. It was also instantly recognisable and impossible to forge. Sailors travelled to the Maldives from around the world to buy the shells. They were traded throughout India, Africa and China, where the earliest written characters for money were based on the shape of a cowrie (贝).

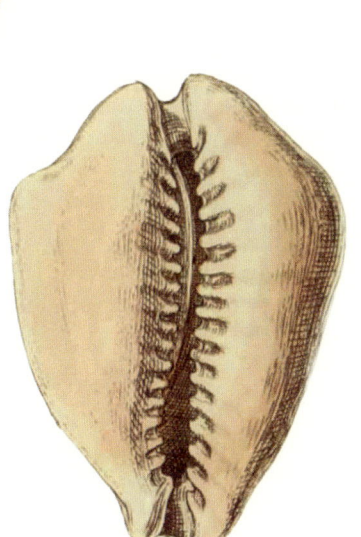

MOLLUSC MONEY
The money cowrie,
Monetaria moneta, lives on
rocky shorelines and feeds
on algae and seaweed.

'Shells rose to exceptional importance in ancient economies around the world'

Psychic Shells

There's something about holding a shell that can inspire a sense of hidden knowledge. Across cultures, shells have long been vessels of spiritual guidance.

Amongst the Ojibwe, or Anishinaabe, who once lived along North America's Atlantic coast, the cowrie – known as the great miigis – carried divine power. Oral tradition tells of a prophecy brought by the shell, urging the people to migrate west to preserve their traditions. They journeyed to what is now Manitoba and Minnesota, bringing cowries with them, and named one of their settlements Whiteshell.

In West Africa, Yoruba priests consult cowries in divination. After honouring the divine spirits, or oshiras, a priest casts sixteen cowries, cut so that both sides are flat, onto a prepared mat, twice. The way they fall – face up or face down – forms one of 256 patterns. Each pattern corresponds to an *odu*, an interpretation that may reveal connections between life and death, answer pressing questions or reveal a guiding oshira.

Cowries play a role in Hindu astrology in Kerala, India. In the ritual of *Prashnam*, 108 money cowries, called *kavidi*, are blessed through prayer. They are each rotated, a portion are separated, and the pattern used to determine a ruling planet, which when compared against a person's horoscope, forms the basis for future predictions.

Today, the involvement of shells in mystical practice is growing. Modern witches turn to *conchomancy* – divination through shells – placing them alongside tarot, crystals and dreams as tools for insight into the unseen.

TIGER COWRIE
Also called the leopard cowrie, *Cypraea tigris* is striped as a subadult and becomes spotted when it matures.

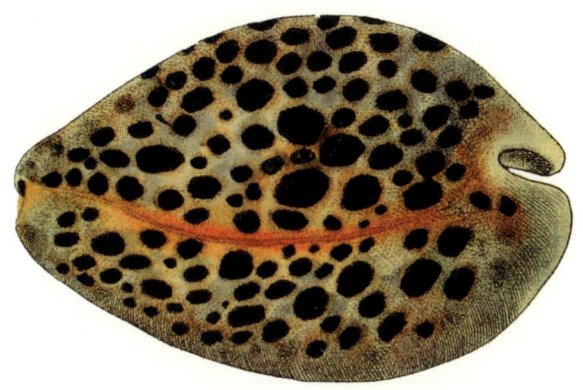

'There's something about holding a shell that can inspire a sense of hidden knowledge'

The Secret Shell

Shell collectors covet shells that are dazzling to look at or hard to find. The rarest shell in the world is both. With a curved form that looks like it's made from highly polished mahogany and black-and-white, zip-like teeth across its opening, fewer than a handful of *Sphaerocypraea incomparabilis* shells are known to exist on land.

The first *Sphaerocypraea incomparabilis* came up in fishing nets in 1963 when the Soviet Union began fishing off the coast of Somalia in deeper waters than had been previously plumbed. A few more were pulled from the depths in subsequent years, but the finds remained secret, held in private collections in the Soviet Union.

'Shell collectors covet shells that are dazzling to look at or hard to find. The rarest shell in the world is both'

'Scientists identified Sphaerocypraea incomparabilis *as a new species belonging to a family presumed extinct for 20 million years*'

Three decades later, a Florida shell dealer got his hands on two of the secret shells. They were eventually donated to the American Museum of Natural History and their existence made public. Scientists identified *Sphaerocypraea incomparabilis* as a new species related to cowries, but belonging to a family presumed extinct for 20 million years.

In 1997, a curator at the museum discovered that one of the two *Sphaerocypraea incomparabilis* had been stolen. The heist was solved by matching a broken tooth on the shell's zip to a picture of a *Sphaerocypraea incomparabilis* shell in a collection in Indonesia. The culprit was a malfeasant appraiser who had been hired by the museum years earlier. He swiped it and sold it for $12,000 to a Belgian collector who, in turn, sold it for $20,000 to a collector in Indonesia. This modern version of conchylomania resolved when the museum got the shell back and the appraiser got time in jail.

Whelks and Conchs

Whelks and conchs are both gastropods with a whirling shell and a large opening called an operculum, which is not so long that it takes up the entire length of the shell like cones or cowries. In other words, they both have conspicuous spires. Despite a seemingly similar shell shape, whelks in the family Buccinidae and conchs in the family Strombidae are very different animals.

Sometimes called 'bullies of the seas' for their predatory ways, whelks have a specialised mouthpart called a radula to bore through the shells of the molluscs that they eat. They have a big muscular foot on which they cruise the seafloor. The umbilicus faces forward and has a groove out of which their nose-like siphon extends. Whelks live in cool, temperate waters and lay their eggs in cases that can look like discarded plastic cords, round bundles or intricate towers.

Meanwhile, conchs – denizens of more tropical seas – are anything but thugs. As herbivores, their radula is specialised to scrape seaweed off rocks. Conchs don't cruise like a garden snail. Instead they dig their tough trapdoor, or operculum, into the sand and use it to vault forward. At the umbilicus of a conch shell is a notch from which the animal extends one of its two stalked eyes.

While the horse conch made this list, it's neither a whelk nor a conch but a tulip snail in the family Fasciolariidae. Like a whelk, it's also a voracious carnivore, known to make a meal of both whelks and conchs.

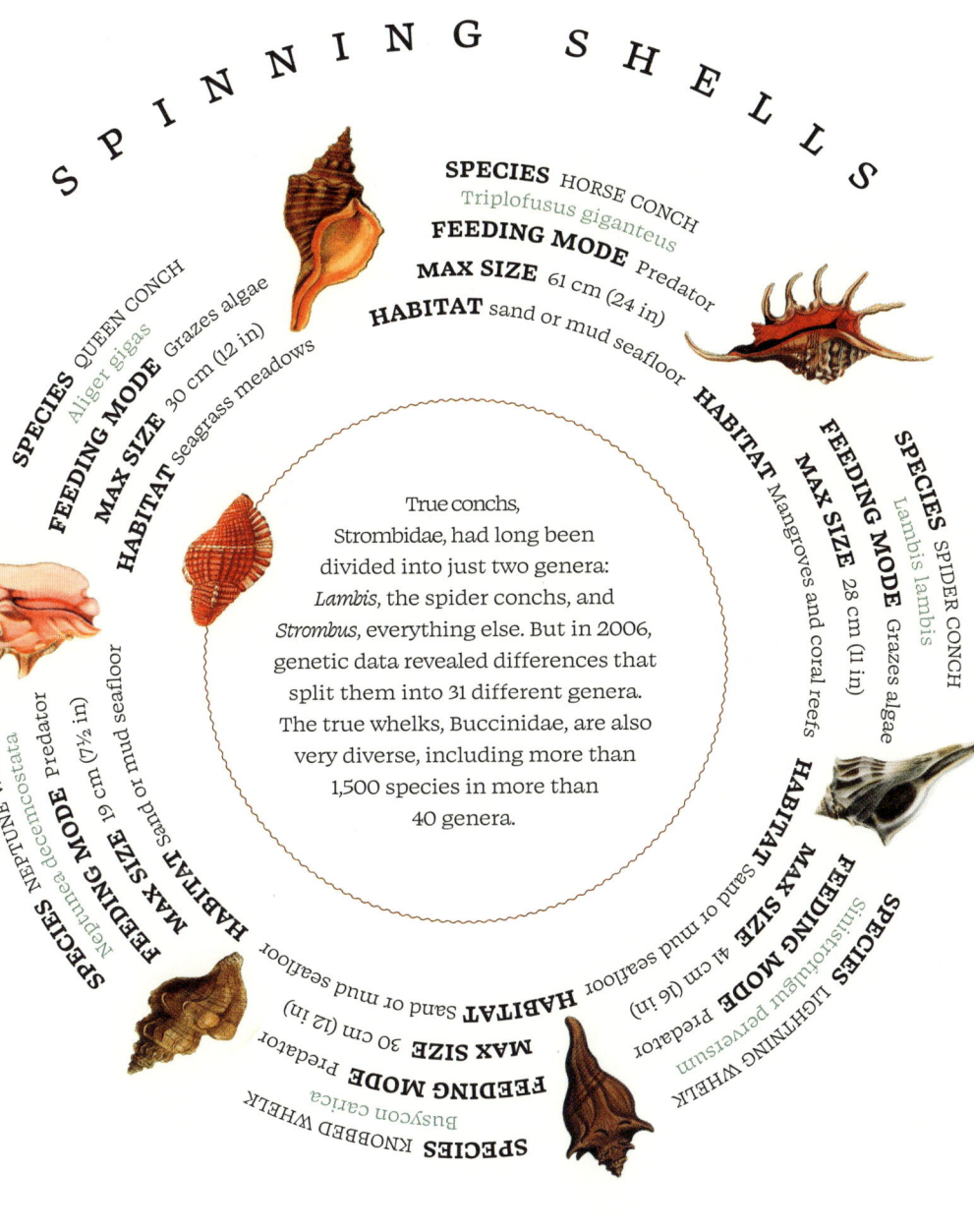

SPECIES HORSE CONCH
Triplofusus giganteus
FEEDING MODE Predator
MAX SIZE 61 cm (24 in)
HABITAT sand or mud seafloor

SPECIES QUEEN CONCH
Aliger gigas
FEEDING MODE Grazes algae
MAX SIZE 30 cm (12 in)
HABITAT Seagrass meadows

SPECIES SPIDER CONCH
Lambis lambis
FEEDING MODE Grazes algae
MAX SIZE 28 cm (11 in)
HABITAT Mangroves and coral reefs

True conchs, Strombidae, had long been divided into just two genera: *Lambis*, the spider conchs, and *Strombus*, everything else. But in 2006, genetic data revealed differences that split them into 31 different genera. The true whelks, Buccinidae, are also very diverse, including more than 1,500 species in more than 40 genera.

SPECIES LIGHTNING WHELK
Sinistrofulgur perversum
FEEDING MODE predator
MAX SIZE 41 cm (16 in)
HABITAT sand or mud seafloor

SPECIES KNOBBED WHELK
Busycon carica
FEEDING MODE Predator
MAX SIZE 30 cm (12 in)
HABITAT Sand or mud seafloor

SPECIES NEPTUNE WHELK
Neptunea decemcostata
FEEDING MODE Predator
MAX SIZE 19 cm (7½ in)
HABITAT Sand or mud seafloor

Through Mollusc Eyes

In terms of the sheer number of types of eyes, no group of animals beats the molluscs. Octopuses have a camera eye like ours, with a pupil, a lens and a retina. So does the giant squid, whose eyes are the largest in the world, the size of dinner plates. In the deep, dark ocean, that great surface maximises absorbed light so it can spot its predator, the sperm whale, a football field away. Meanwhile, nautiluses have just a pinhole that lets light in. Snails have eyes that are cup-shaped, usually on the ends of tentacles.

A scallop has up to 200 eyes. Light passes through a pupil that can dilate and contract, then it hits two retinas and a concave mirror made of guanine crystals, which focuses the light on the edges of the retina. It's a similar structure to advanced telescopes and means scallops can form images, so they know when to jet away from danger.

Ark clams have compound eyes, which form many versions of the same image, similar to insects. The giant clam (*Tridacna* spp.) has hundreds of ocelli – very simple eyes all around the edge of its massive shell.

Eyes have evolved probably fifty different times in animals, leading to wildly different types of seeing. But scientists are beginning to speculate that the molecules which detect light – opsins – might all come from the pressure to protect against damage to cells from ultraviolet light. If true, this is an example of how by looking at diversity, we can discover the connections between us.

WINGS AND EYES
The turkey wing ark clam, *Arca zebra*, has many compound eyes that act as an optical alarm system signalling to snap shut when danger approaches.

THE SECRET WORLD OF SHELLS

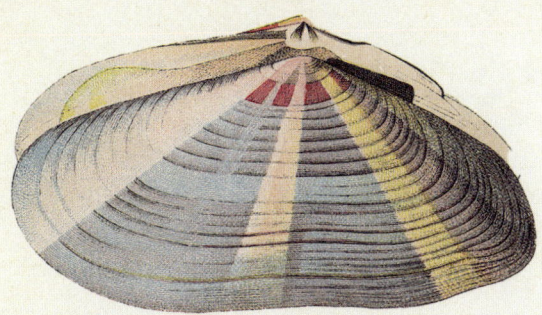

BIODIVERSE BIVALVES
These bivalves include
clams and mussels that
live in both fresh water
and the sea, from the
Indo-Pacific to Siberia.

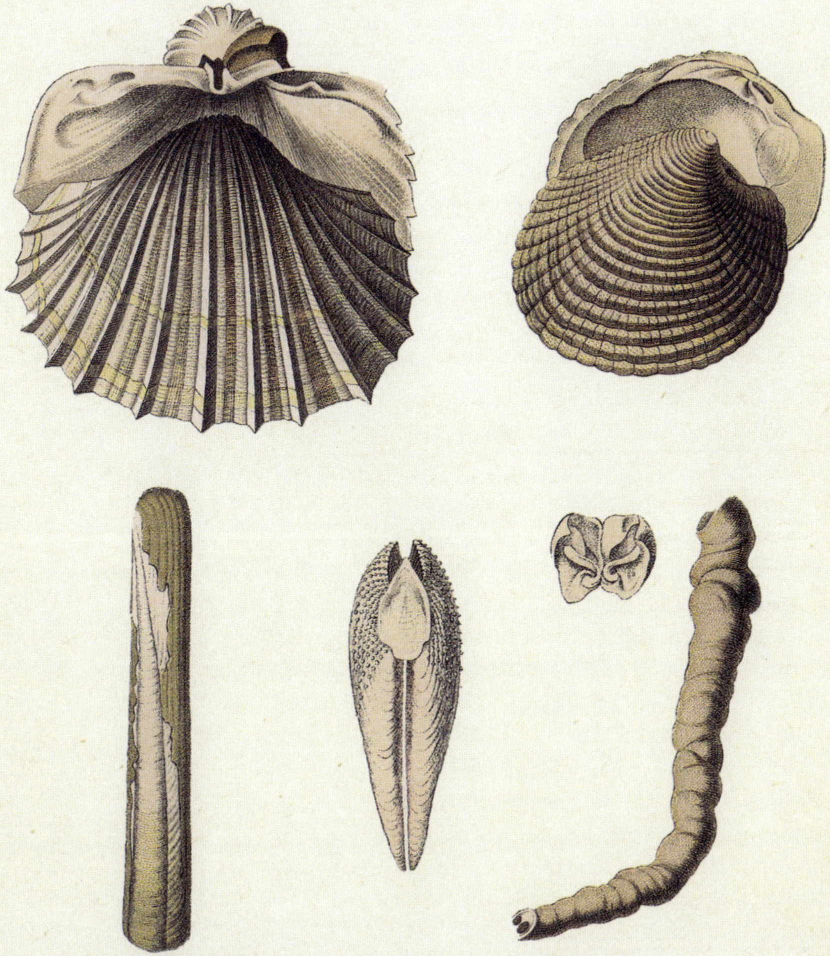

THE SECRET WORLD OF SHELLS

Traces of Time

Sometimes you can be far from the sea and find a seashell. You might be on the top of a mountain or deep in the forest. How did it get there?

Shells may be the most commonly fossilised objects on earth. Because they are hard, they can withstand geologic pressures that destroy soft body parts. Sometimes water flowing through pores in shells deposit minerals like silica, making them even harder. In other cases, the shell might be dissolved but replaced with minerals such as pyrite or quartz, leaving a shell-shaped mineral mould. Over the millennia, tectonic forces lifted the ancient oceans and with them the fossilised shells of the animals that lived there, depositing them on mountaintops and in forests.

Bivalves, like clams and oysters, are often fossilised and are fairly easy to identify because they look like their living relatives. A snail called turritella, with a long, pointed, tightly coiled shell, is one of the most common fossil gastropods.

Ammonites, which have chambered coiled shells similar to the nautilus, are found in fossil deposits worldwide. Their cousins, belemnites and orthoceras, also have chambered shells but they are straight and long. Shelled cephalopods dominated the seas between 240 and 65 million years ago.

Other common fossil shells belong to ancient echinoderms called crinoids that grew on a stalk. Ancient sharks, like our modern ones, shed teeth regularly. So, if you find yourself in a marine fossil bed, look for some of those ancient teeth, too.

ANCIENT ARTISTRY
Naturalist and artist Ernst Haeckel depicted the external ornamentation and internal complexity (lower centre) of ammonite shells.

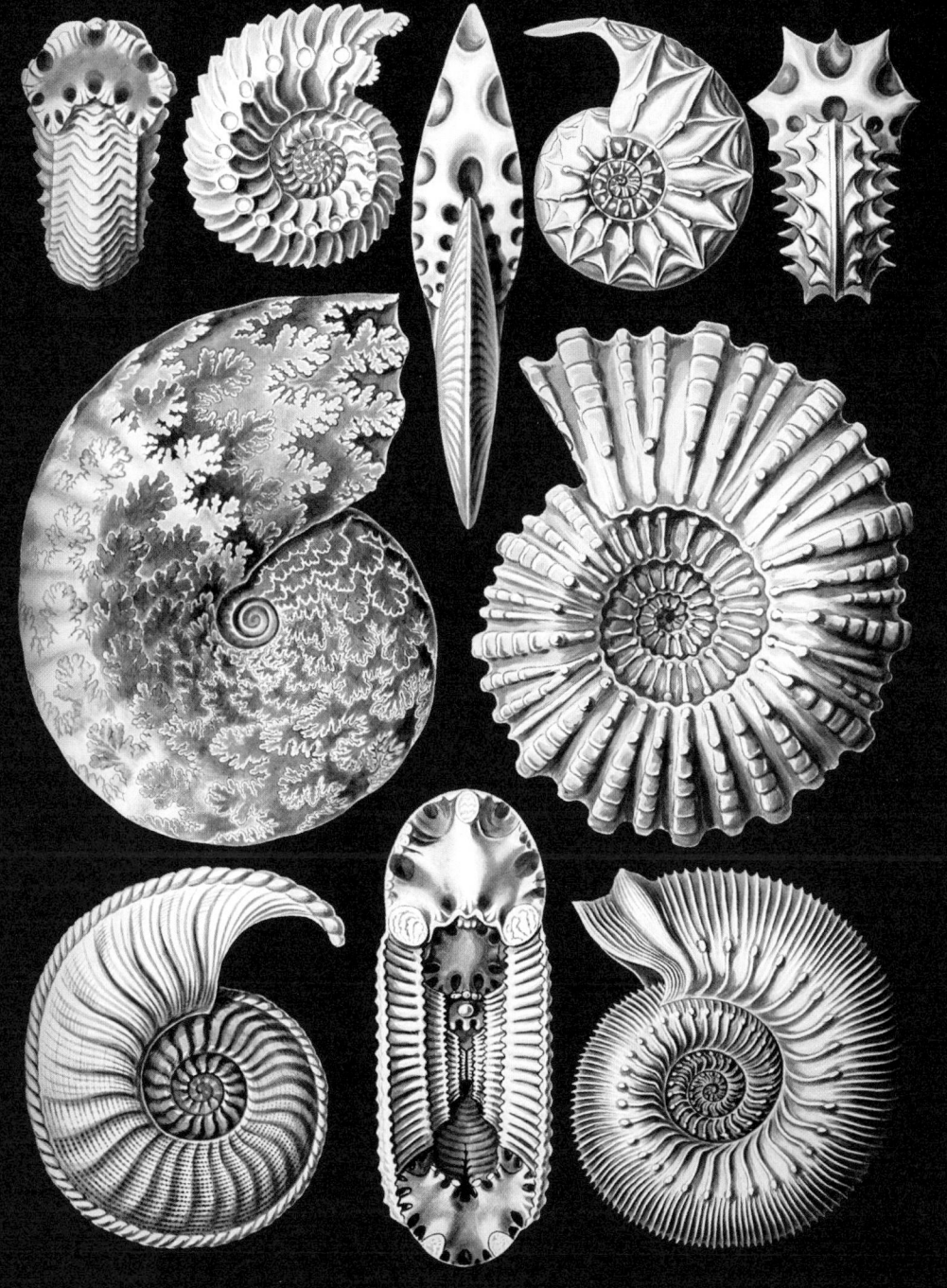

'Fossil shells are more than the remains of an animal; they are a recording of the sea's history'

Fossil shells are more than the remains of an animal; they are a recording of the sea's history. When animals make shells, they incorporate the minerals that surround them. Environmental conditions, like temperature, influence how that happens. For example, oxygen exists in two different isotopes: oxygen-18 and oxygen-16. If a fossil shell contains more oxygen-18, it indicates that the water was cooler when the shell was formed. Carbon, the molecule that is the basis for all life on our planet, also exists in isotopes. The isotope carbon-14 can be used to accurately date fossils back to about 60,000 years. For older fossils, other elements' isotopes can be used but with less precision.

Paleontologists call a group of different shells that have fossilised together an assemblage, because they are a record of which kinds of animals lived together in ancient ecosystems. An assemblage with just a few species indicates an environment that has gone through a period of stress. One with a lot of diversity signals health and complexity. In any assemblage, paleontologists particularly prize finding certain ancient animals, called index fossils. These creatures lived over vast stretches of the seas but for just a short period of time. Their presence provides a geological timestamp for surrounding fossils.

By studying the information recorded in fossil shells, scientists can begin to piece together the sea's ancient ecosystems, and the oceanic conditions in which they existed, so that we can better understand our planet's past and use that information to tell us about our future.

OCEANS OF CHANGE
Although extinct today, cephalopods called ammonites, whose coiled shells occur in fossil deposits, once dominated marine ecosystems.

THE SECRET WORLD OF SHELLS

FISHING CONES
Some cone snails, including the striated cone (*Conus striatus*), fire a harpoon and reel it in to capture fish.

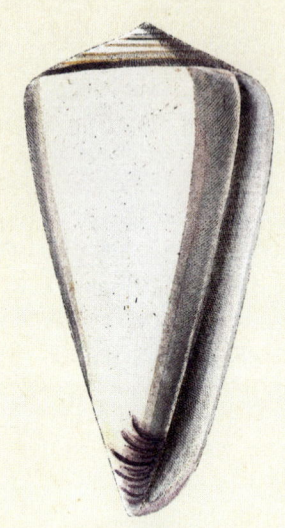

THE SECRET WORLD OF SHELLS

Shells on a Mountain

In 1665, as formalised science was getting started in Europe, the ability to perform dissections gained stature. This played to the talents of a young Danish man named Nicholas Steno (1638–86) who was gifted with the scalpel. As a medical student, he made pioneering discoveries about the heart muscle and the parotid duct in the mouth. These advances garnered the attention of the Grand Duke of Tuscany, Ferdinand II, who offered Steno a cushy position to study the natural world.

In Tuscany, Steno took long walks through the mountains where he noticed stones that looked like shells. At the time, people believed that stones grew in the soil, much as mushrooms or mosses. As evidence: every year farmers cleared their fields of stones and every year they found new ones in the soil. To Steno, the shells on the tops of the mountains looked too much like those on the seashore. He made a massive intellectual leap recognising that the shells on the mountains had been alive once, just like the molluscs in the sea. When they died, they were covered in layer after layer of sediment. Later, the sediment layers were deformed, becoming mountains. These theories formed the foundation of modern geology and Steno's principles of stratigraphy are still taught today.

Steno found himself struggling to reconcile his discoveries with religious teachings and spent the rest of his life in poverty and service to God in a monastery in Germany. The masterful study on the meaning of ancient shells was Steno's last scientific work.

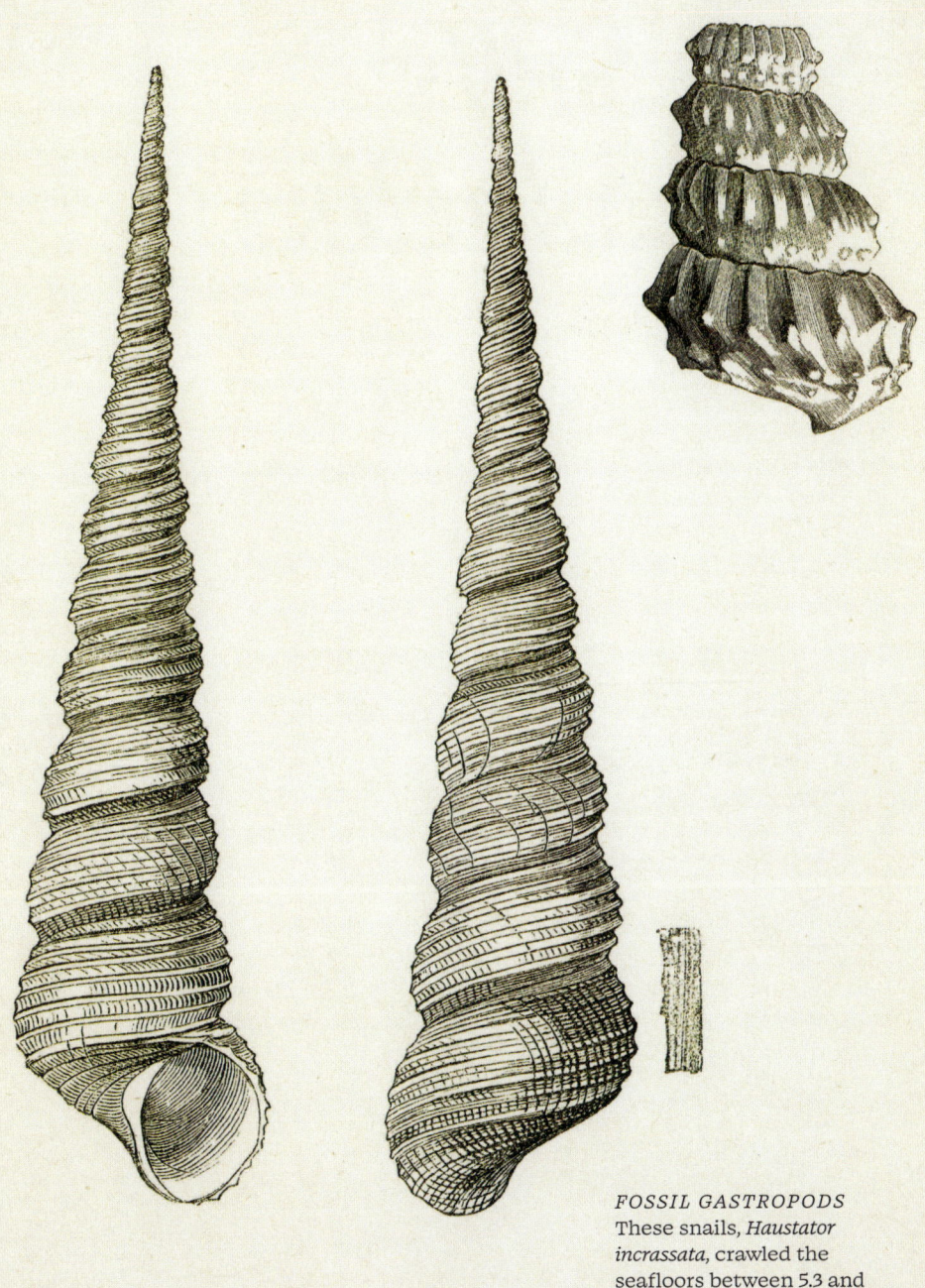

FOSSIL GASTROPODS
These snails, *Haustator incrassata*, crawled the seafloors between 5.3 and 2.6 million years ago.

She Sells Seashells

Since picking up this book, you might have been tempted to chant, 'She sells sea shells by the seashore.' This tongue twister is more than just fun to say. It celebrates a real woman who indeed made a living selling fossil shells on the coast of Dorset, England, in the nineteenth century.

Mary Anning (1799–1847) was the daughter of a cabinetmaker who augmented his income by selling curios such as snakestones (ammonites) and devils'-fingers (belemnites) dug from the nearby cliffs – home to rich Jurassic marine fossil beds. By the time Mary was 12, she was making extraordinary finds. With her brother, she discovered a large, complete skeleton of an ichthyosaur, an ancient swimming dinosaur, which sold at auction for £23.

Despite having little formal education, Anning became a world expert in fossils. She supported herself with a shop that drew celebrated paleontologists from around the world, and she made great contributions to the field herself. She discovered the first British flying dinosaur – a pterosaur displayed in the British Museum – and identified a new species of ancient shark. She also discovered that coprolite was actually fossilised feces.

Despite having more knowledge of fossils than many men of the time, as a woman, Anning was banned from presenting her own work. She had to ask men to publish her findings, and many either failed to acknowledge her contributions or claimed them for their own. Nonetheless, Anning is recognised as a pioneering scientist. Now, when you hear the poem, perhaps you'll remember her too.

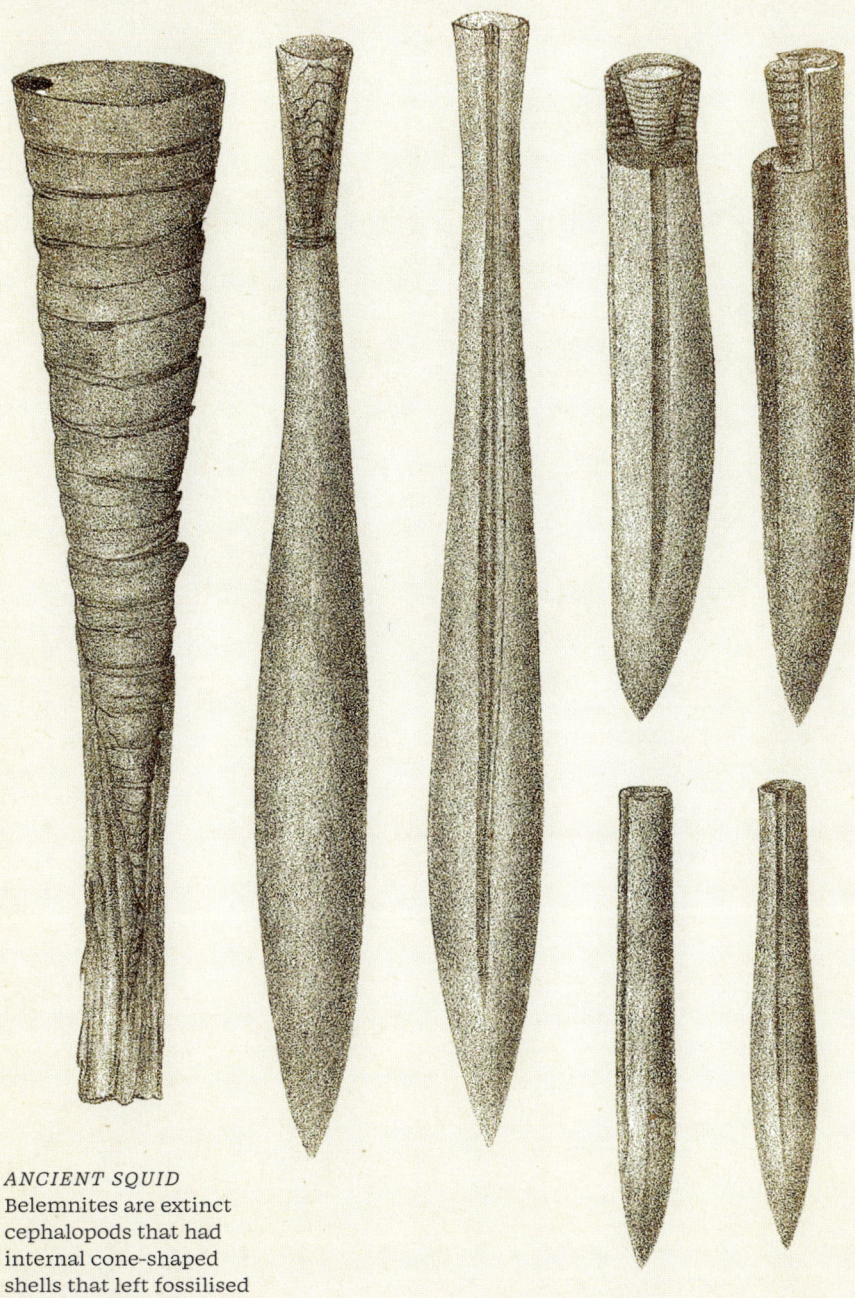

ANCIENT SQUID
Belemnites are extinct
cephalopods that had
internal cone-shaped
shells that left fossilised
remains like these
in New Zealand.

LIGHTNING TURBAN
Also known as the
common warrener,
Lunella undulata is
endemic to Australia
where it is often found
in archaeological sites.

Glowing Molluscs

Up on sunlit land, if we want to transmit information long distances, we yell or call, whistle or roar. But the ocean grows dimmer and dimmer with depth, so light becomes one of the most powerful ways to send a signal. In fact, creating your own light, a process called bioluminescence, may be the most common language in the sea.

Half of the classes of molluscs can produce bioluminescence. They emit light from special structures called photophores or light organs. In many of these animals, the light is produced by luminescent bacteria that the molluscs cultivate like crops.

Cephalopods are the most masterful of the mollusc light-makers. In these motile animals, the flashes of light scare away predators, attract prey and act as a form of communication with each other.

Shelled molluscs can also shine. Planaxid snails gather between rocks during low tide. With a similar shape to periwinkles, and perhaps because they blink on and off like a flashing camera, they are called clusterwinks. Their shell acts like a diffuser, spreading out the light so predators think the snails are bigger than they are.

The glowing piddock is another famous bioluminescent bivalve. Greek naturalist Pliny the Elder noted that eating these molluscs raw turns into a party trick because they 'glitter both in the mouth of persons masticating them and in their hands, and even on the floor and on their clothes when drops fall on them ... their juice possesses a property that we should marvel.'

ANGEL WINGS
Members of Pholadidae,
called angel wings
or piddocks, have toothed
shells on one side for
burrowing into clay
or rocks.

'Bioluminescence may be the most common language in the sea'

Toxic Beauty

With more than 500 species, the genus *Conus*, or cone snails, may be the marine world's largest. Appearing in the fossil record about 55 million years ago, cone snails live in tropical oceans, mostly in the Indian and western Pacific oceans, though they range to the eastern Pacific as well.

This tropic-loving group is confined to the coral reefs and the adjacent sandy seafloor, a somewhat limited habitat by the ocean's standards. So, it's curious that cone snails exhibit much diversity. The explanation comes from the great biodiversity of coral ecosystems themselves. Taking up less than 1 percent of the ocean's area, coral reefs support a quarter of all marine life, some 830,000 species.

Cone snails exploit this vast range of food: some eat worms, some eat other molluscs and others are even capable of snagging fish. Cone snails aren't fast but they make up for speed with powerful weaponry. They have an organ called a proboscis, which is like a nose and mouth that's equipped with injectable venom, and a modified radula that functions as teeth, tongue and spear.

Each of the hundreds of cone snail species have evolved a unique toxic cocktail consisting of dozens of different molecules, mostly short chains of peptides. They block the transfer of ions into and out of animal cells. These venoms are some of the ocean's richest biochemical innovations and are being actively investigated as the source of new pharmaceuticals.

Be warned: The venom in a cone snail affects humans too. Never pick up a live cone snail!

VENOMOUS CONES

SPECIES GLORY-OF-THE-SEA CONE
Conus gloriamaris
MAX DEPTH 300 m (984 ft)
MAX SIZE 61 cm (24 in)
RANGE Indo-Pacific Ocean

SPECIES ALPHABET CONE
Conus spurius
MAX DEPTH 30 m (98 ft)
MAX SIZE 8 cm (3 in)
RANGE Caribbean Sea

SPECIES CAT CONE
Conus catus
MAX DEPTH 73 m (24 ft)
MAX SIZE 5 cm (2 in)
RANGE Indo-Pacific Ocean

Like bitter Monarch butterflies and venomous tree frogs, cone snails' bright colours might warn predators of their dangerous weaponry. Smaller cone snails' stabs won't hurt more than a bee sting. But the geography cone is also known as the cigarette snail because there's just time for one cigarette before its toxin becomes fatal.

SPECIES CLOTH OF GOLD CONE
Conus textile
MAX DEPTH 50 m (164 ft)
MAX SIZE 9 cm (3½ in)
RANGE Indo-Pacific Ocean

SPECIES MAGICAL CONE
Conus magus
MAX DEPTH 100 m (328 ft)
MAX SIZE 9 cm (3½ in)
RANGE Indo-Pacific Ocean

SPECIES GEOGRAPHY CONE
Conus geographus
MAX DEPTH 20 m (65 ft)
MAX SIZE 15 cm (6 in)
RANGE Indo-Pacific Ocean

A Treasured Shell

Until the mid-twentieth century, the most expensive shell in the world was *Conus gloriamaris*, the glory-of-the-sea cone. With a distinctive brown and white pattern of interlocking V's, a single shell could easily sell for thousands of dollars. But in 1969, this cone snail's habitat was discovered, and prices for the shell fell to just a few hundred dollars.

No longer valuable for its rarity, today *Conus gloriamaris* – along with other members of its genus – are prized for another reason: their toxins. It's thought that each species of cone snail contains as many as 200 pharmacologically active components. With more than 500 species, the biodiversity of compounds with potential medical value reaches the tens of thousands. The value of these chemicals to heal human ailments could be priceless.

Conotoxins, the name given to molecules in a cone snail's venom, are interesting to researchers because they are highly potent and specifically target particular cell receptors. One of the chemicals in the geography cone snail (*Conus geographus*) toxin mimics a hormone that lowers the blood sugar of their prey, causing them to swim more slowly. It's being studied as a treatment for diabetes. Ziconotide, already available as a pharmaceutical, is a synthetic form of a chemical made by the cone snail *Conus magus*. It interferes with neurotransmitters and is used to treat pain resistant to other therapies. Other conotoxins are being investigated for their use as anti-epileptic treatments, to stop nerve-cell death after stroke or spinal cord injury, and to detect lung cancer.

MARBLED CONES
Conus marmoreus is a
type species. Regardless
of how science changes,
the moniker *Conus*
will remain with the
marbled cone.

The Gift
of Shells

In the Trobriand Islands of the western Pacific, shells are at the centre of an ancient ritual that has taught the people who understand it much about the meaning of gifts. The archipelago is made up of eighteen islands forming an elongated oval. People risk their lives to travel hundreds of miles by canoe across the waves to give gifts of necklaces adorned with spiny oyster (*Spondylus* spp.) shells, polished into red discs, and white armbands decorated with the polished top of a cone shell (*Conus millepunctatus*).

These items are passed from person to person in formal rituals, with the necklaces moving around the archipelago in a anticlockwise direction and the armbands clockwise. The exchanges never happen at the same time. Rather someone waits until they have received an item of similar value to what they received and then voyages to give it as a gift. Also, a gift never remains with someone for long; arrangements must be made to give it away to the right person soon after receiving it. The flow of gifts is seen as two streams in constant motion in opposite directions.

Polish anthropologist Bronislaw Malinowski visited the Trobriand Islands in the early 1910s and brought attention to these gift-giving traditions in the book *Argonauts of the Western Pacific*. Malinowski likened the giving to the Greek story of Jason seeking the Golden Fleece, wherein, like the fleece, the gifts themselves have little inherent value. Instead, it is their voyage that imbues them with meaning.

THORNY OYSTER
Spondylus tenuis isn't
closely related to true
oysters. Like a scallop,
it has many eyes around
the edge of its mantle.

TIMELESS TREASURE
The names of the
species are illegible in
this plate from a 1757
volume, but the shells'
beauty is enduring.

The Meaning of Shells

Stones have long been assigned meanings. Purple amethysts are thought to bring calm and relaxation; black obsidian repels negativity. Similarly, shells can also inspire particular significance affiliated with their shape or the behaviour of the animals who built them. Although meanings are in the mind of the beholder, perhaps one of the shells below will express a feeling or idea you might want to share with someone you care about:

Abalones, amongst the largest gastropods, are said to represent strength, balance and abundance.

Clams, two shells of similar sizes connected together, symbolise balance, communication, love and protecting secrets.

Conchs, their sturdy form prized as a resonant wind instrument, typify communication, structure, leadership and harmony.

Cone shells, made by animals that strike with venom, signify competition, control, cutting ties and dangerous beauty.

Cowries, their shine and curves associated with femininity, represent prosperity, fertility, the sacred and divination.

Limpets, found in groups, their flattened form ideal for clinging, are known for tenacity, endurance, and also community and family.

Moon snails, also called shark's eyes, represent intuition, deception, the subconscious and cycles.

Mussels, attached by intertwining byssal threads to the surface on which they live, correspond to networking, risk-taking, adaptability and individuality.

Nautilus shells, whose chambers follow mathematical logic, depict order, expansion and higher consciousness.

Oysters, which sometimes contain pearls, are symbolic of inner beauty, healing, protection and introspection.

Scallops, whose elegant, fan-like form coalesces in a single point, denote love, beauty, healing and the journey to find meaning.

HINGED HARMONY
Clams like these, whose paired shells are joined together by a hinge, can represent connection and safe-keeping.

The Art of the Shell

Since ancient times, seashells have been both subjects of art and incorporated into the works themselves. The first engraving was a zigzag made on a shell half a million years ago by our cousin *Homo erectus*. As long ago as 75,000 years, Paleolithic people in Israel, Algeria, Morocco and South Africa made shell beads from small nassa mud snails. Around 10,000 years ago, Egyptians used shells in jewellery and ritual practices, as did people in Mesopotamia and the Indus Valley, at the same time that people in Mesoamerica carved conchs into horns and ritual objects.

Ancient Greeks and Romans frequently used shells in mosaics. Unearthed in Rome in 2023, a banquet hall built 2,300 years ago is decorated with a gorgeous compilation of seashells, coral, glass and marble that depicts vines, mythical sea creatures and Roman battles.

The Renaissance saw a resurgence of shell mosaics, along with carving shells into cameos. Visual representation of shells also came into fashion. Amongst the most famous is the etching of a marbled cone, 'The Shell (*Conus Marmoreus*)' by Rembrandt van Rijn (1606–69). At 6 cm (2½ in) it is roughly the same size as the shell itself, which was part of a large collection of shells listed on a 1656 inventory from the artist's house.

Another painter of the Dutch Renaissance, Adriaen Coorte (1665–1707) focused on shells. His works' careful detail created a three-dimensionality on the canvas. Often set against a dark background, his use of light came to typify still-life painting.

ART APPRECIATION
This 1696 painting by
Adriaen Coorte, *Still Life
with Two Large and Three
Small Shells on a Slab of
Stone*, hangs in the Louvre.

In the 1700s, a playfully elegant artistic style swept through Europe: Rococo – the word is derived from the French *rocaille*, meaning rock and shellwork. Swirling forms of scallops and snails adorned furniture, architecture, silver, ceramics and plasterwork. Even wigs looked like large gastropods piled on top of women's heads. Nineteenth-century Victorians tamed the shell craze somewhat, but shells were still incorporated into items of art, often in the form of highly decorated boxes used as keepsakes. Mrs Roberson's shop in London's Grosvenor Square sold packets of shells sorted by size and colour, as well as patterns for box designs for society women to use in their art.

As the century drew to a close, German naturalist Ernst Haeckel coupled scientific detail with artistic elegance in *Kunstformen der Natur* (Art Forms in Nature), a spectacular collection of lithographic prints of plants and animals, especially shells. His style, which depicted nature as rhythmic patterns, helped birth the Art Nouveau movement.

The twentieth century burst open the symmetrical lines of Art Nouveau. Semi-abstract modern artist Georgia O'Keeffe used the form of shells as a reference to sexuality, their similarity to genitalia made overt in paintings such as *Slightly Open Clam Shell* (1926) and *Two Pink Shells/Pink Shell* (1937). In the 1940s and 1950s, surrealist Salvador Dalí used the motif of shells suspended in mid-air as a reference to fragility in the wake of the deployment of atomic bombs. Shells remain a potent artistic motif today, symbolising both the delight and wonder of nature as well as challenges to our planet's health.

'In the 1700s, a playfully elegant artistic style swept through Europe: Rococo – the word is derived from the French rocaille, meaning rock and shellwork'

COMB-GILLED SNAILS
The beautiful gastropods in this lithograph by Ernst Haeckel grow asymmetrically, so one gill is enlarged and looks like a comb.

Micromolluscs

We humans have a fondness for tiny things. Babies, puppies, kittens, small-scaled houses, model trains, even fun-size sweets are all delightful. Microshells, every bit as captivating, deserve a spot on that list.

While there's no consensus on what qualifies as a microshell, any adult mollusc that's less than about 8 mm (¼ in) likely falls into the category – and lots do. Microshells occur in about twenty-four different mollusc families.

Amongst the world's smallest shells is *Condylonucula maya*, in the family Nuculidae, which grows to 0.5 mm Shells in the family Omalogyridae are also diminutive at less than 1 mm in size. Microshells have a breathtaking array of diversity from teeny tulip forms to minute hinged valves, each as finely whorled, banded and spired as the shells of their larger cousins. Though diminutive, micromolluscs play critical roles in food webs, filtering seawater and as prey.

Microshells are hard to see and study. Our fingers are too big to pick them up easily, so we have to use tweezers or the hairs on a sable brush to collect them. Observing their fine detail requires a hand lens or dissecting microscope. Because of these challenges, they have been overlooked by scientists, likely leading to an underestimate of mollusc biodiversity. One careful study found that of more than 2,500 mollusc species in New Caledonia's tropical ocean, micromolluscs made up more than one-third. These minute molluscs remind us to look at the world a little closer.

PYRAMID SHELLS
The tiny snails in the family Pyramidellidae are less than 1.3 cm (½ in) and mostly parasitise worms, molluscs and crustations.

THE SECRET WORLD OF SHELLS

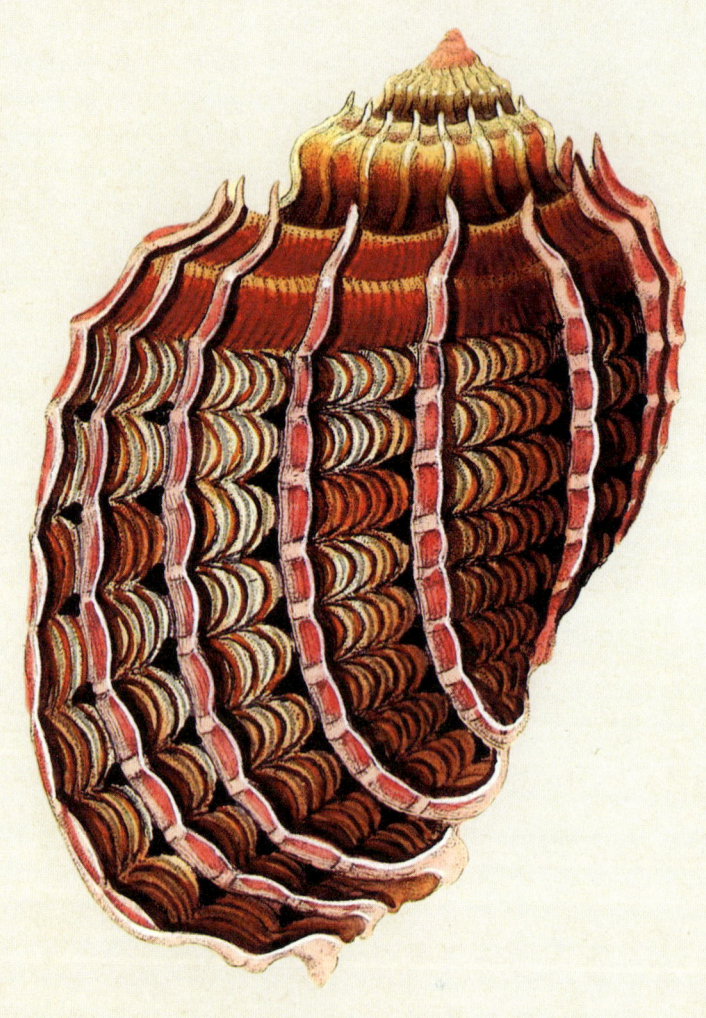

NOBLE HARP
Harpa harpa, a 10-cm (4-in)
predatory gastropod, is
found in the tropical
Indian and Pacific oceans.

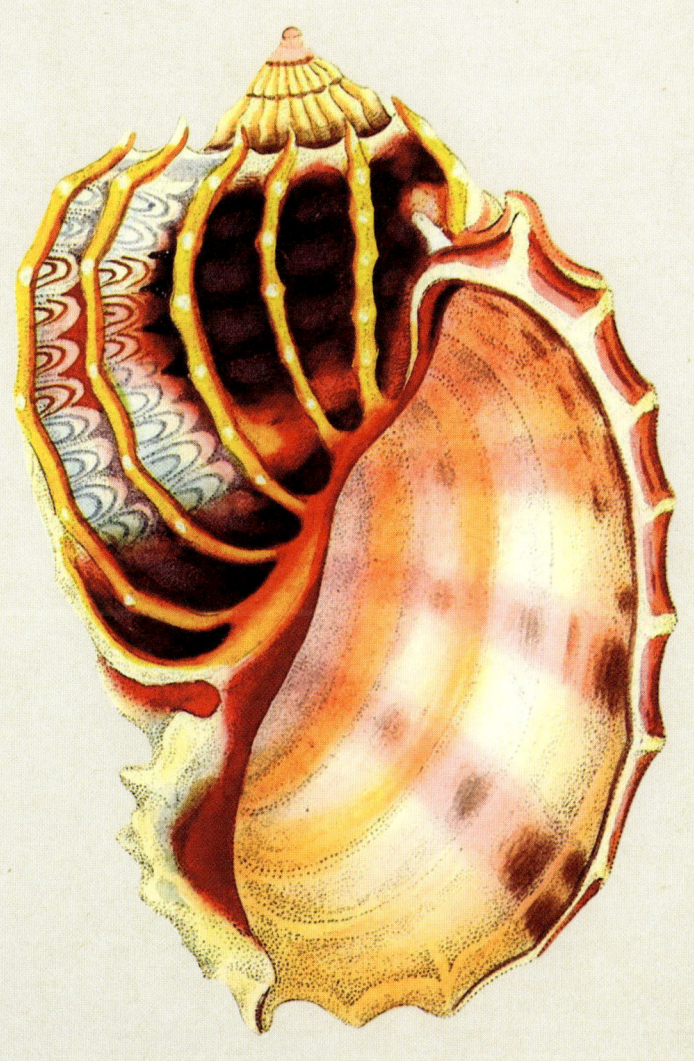

Seashells and the Sea

It's easy to appreciate a shell for its beauty and elegance, but it's also important to zoom out and consider the larger impact of shells on the sea. As a source of sand, seashells stabilise seafloors. In places where there are oyster and mussel beds, they significantly reduce erosion. The corrugated surface of shells provides a rich habitat that supports biological diversity. Shells also regulate the ocean's chemistry. They store and release calcium carbonate, which keeps the pH of the ocean in check. The carbon that shells contain is also a natural storage mechanism, which offsets our emissions from burning fossil fuels.

Yet, shell-making molluscs face challenges in today's seas. Warming temperatures depress mollusc growth rates. Ocean acidification, a second consequence of burning fossil fuels, makes the chemistry of shell-building more difficult. Overharvesting depletes mollusc population sizes and pollution can further diminish reproduction rates. Dredging and coastal development raze mollusc habitats. As our shipping systems become more global, invasive species and disease cause further population declines.

Owing to their extraordinary diversity and massive population sizes, molluscs remain integral to marine ecosystems, both as prey and as predators. Capable of purifying enormous quantities of seawater, they are like the sea's great filtration system, performing that critical service day in and day out. Through our admiration for seashells, which we express in ritual and art, in our fisheries and by discovering them on the beach, shells will always connect us to the world's oceans on which we so deeply depend.

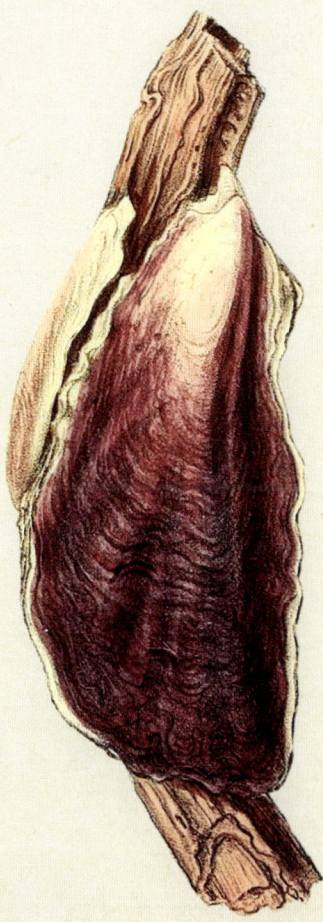

*ECOSYSTEM
ENGINEERS*
Oysters like these clean
and filter seawater, create
abundant habitat and
provide food for others,
including humans.

3

Nature's Masterpieces: Thirty Shells

Queen Conch

ALIGER GIGAS

CLASS
Gastropoda

RANGE
Caribbean

HABITAT
Seagrass meadows to
depths of 35 m (115 ft)

SIZE
Up to 30 cm (12 in)

OF NOTE
Important as Caribbean
food, instrument

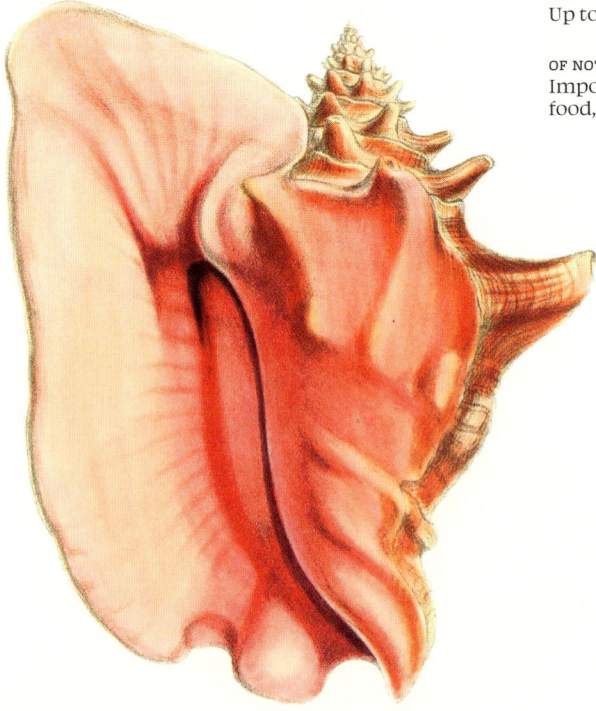

DISCOVER MORE

With a crown of nine to eleven spiked whorls and a royal, cape-like wing, the queen conch is an apt English name for this iconic Caribbean snail. It also goes by many Spanish monikers: *caracol rosado* (pink conch), *caracol de las Indias* (conch of the Indies) and *caracol del Caribe* (conch of the Caribbean). In the Indigenous Arawak language, it is known as *fotuto*, referring to the shell's use as a trumpet. A hole drilled into the top of the shell forms a mouthpiece for a rich, ancient tone that has sounded across the seas for generations.

In its youth, the queen conch has a largely unadorned conic shape and a sharp edge along its lip. Locals in Florida call such shells 'rollers' because the waves roll them across the seafloor. As the queen conch matures, its outer lip begins to thicken and extend into an extravagant flare. Over time, the asymmetry makes it impossible for waves to overturn the animal.

It's unclear how such a massive covering plays a role in the queen conch's unusual locomotion. Rather than slide across the sand like a garden snail, the queen conch anchors the back part of its foot bearing the hard lip in the sand. Then it lifts the front part of its foot and hurls itself forward. This motion has been likened to pole-vaulting and it's suggested that leaving the ground momentarily may be a way to throw predators off its scent. The leaping ability also makes the queen conch an excellent climber, even capable of scaling concrete walls.

Queen conch meat is integral to Caribbean fare: slightly chewy, sweet and mild. But the culinary appeal has taken a toll. In the British Virgin Islands, there's a spot where so many conch shells have been tossed that they form a dune island rising 20 m (66 ft) above the seafloor, a visual account of 800 years of harvest. In 2024, queen conch was listed as 'threatened' under the US Endangered Species Act, and fishing is now illegal in Florida. Where awareness of this plight is growing, fisherpeople are working with scientists to develop fishing seasons and size limits to support healthy populations of these regal gastropods.

2 *Juno's Snail*

SCAPHELLA JUNONIA

CLASS
Gastropoda

RANGE
Caribbean

HABITAT
Sand or mud seafloor to
depths of 110 m (361 ft)

SIZE
Up to 15 cm (6 in)

OF NOTE
Subject of a collecting craze

DISCOVER MORE

Juno's snail has an elegant, spindle-shaped shell with a smooth aperture that may have teeth along a short section of its length. The whorls leading to the shell's point have an interesting texture, not unlike a thumbprint. The shell is patterned in square dots of different colours – blue, red and purple on a cream-coloured canvas.

Long considered one of the rarest finds, junonia, as many in Florida call it, is revealing itself more often these days. The slight increase in the possibility of finding one has sparked a collecting craze. Some speculate that deeper seafloor dredging may be dislodging the snails from their deepwater habitat, or perhaps stronger storms and hurricanes scour the seafloor and kick the shells ashore. Finding a Juno's snail has taken on mythical qualities and collectors describe the search as an almost spiritual experience, stating: 'The shell will find you when it's ready.'

Where the snail's divine name came from is up for debate. Sources claim it was either named for the goddess Juno, protector of home and women, or the bird of Juno (the peacock). Perhaps the animal's canary-yellow foot with vivid black splotches in combination with the polka-dotted shell was behind that choice of appellation.

The range of Juno's snail extends from Florida to Texas and Mexico and includes two subspecies. *Scaphella junonia butleri* is found off Mexico's Yucatan Peninsula. Its shell is a lighter cream and has smaller spots and it looks like a sun-faded version of Juno's snail. *Scaphella junonia johnstoneae* has spots that are darker and closer together than Juno's snail.

This subspecies lives exclusively off the coast of Alabama and was named for that state's most famous amateur conchologist, Kathleen Yerger Johnstone (1906–96). Johnstone was a dance teacher who made shelling popular by giving speeches and writing books on seashells. In 1990, she became even more celebrated when her namesake was declared the state shell.

'Should the wise legislators of Alabama decide to take meaningful public relations action, I hope their choice will be an attractive shell that is unique to the waters of Alabama', said Tucker Abbott, director of the Shell Museum and Educational Foundation, Inc. at the time. 'I can think of no more appropriate shell than the beautiful Johnstone's Junonia.'

3

Red Abalone

HALIOTIS RUFESCENS

CLASS
Gastropoda

RANGE
Pacific

HABITAT
Rocky shorelines to depths
of 180 m (590 ft)

SIZE
Up to 30 cm (12 in)

OF NOTE
Iconic on the US West Coast;
farming and illegal trade
in meat

DISCOVER MORE

Perhaps the most iconic species of the US Pacific Northwest, the domed shell of the red abalone can span 30 cm (12 in). Its top surface, tinted rose, is often mossy-looking. In fact, it's a habitat itself, home to seaweeds, sponges, barnacles and other molluscs. As many as ninety gastropod species have been documented living on top of abalone shells. The characteristic holes that curve across the shell's surface are used for respiration, filling in succession as the animal grows. Its foot is yellowish, and as it creeps along the seafloor, tentacles with eyes on the ends peek from beneath the shell. The large, powerful foot creates suction, so that strong waves or predators such as crabs, octopuses, sea otters and people struggle to dislodge it. If the animal no longer inhabits the shell, the inside is a rainbow of iridescence.

For more than 12,000 years, people have used abalone shells, first as food but also for tools, decoration and ceremony. In the eighteenth century, the Spanish traded fur for abalone. In the nineteenth century, abalone was shipped in bulk to Asia, where it was a delicacy on menus.

Over time, red abalone declined in abundance, and regulators limited harvests. By 2014, 2.5 cm (1 in) of red abalone meat could sell for $2,000 per pound. Unsurprisingly, a dangerous black market evolved. Diving for abalone exposes one to cold, entanglement and encounters with marine life, all exacerbated when the taking is done illegally. Abalone diving claimed a dozen lives a year.

While overfishing was one problem, an ecological chain reaction dealt a harsher blow. A 2014 heatwave killed 90 percent of California's bull kelp and collapsed sunflower starfish populations. Sunflower starfish prey on purple sea urchins, which, in turn, graze bull kelp, a favourite food of abalone. With no predators, purple urchin populations exploded and outcompeted abalone for whatever bull kelp remained. By 2017, the red abalone were starving. A year later, the abalone fishery was closed entirely.

Today, red abalone are listed as critically endangered, but up on land, people are developing skills to raise the animals in tanks. Enterprising marine aquarists are growing red abalone, and perhaps building a future for the legendary molluscs.

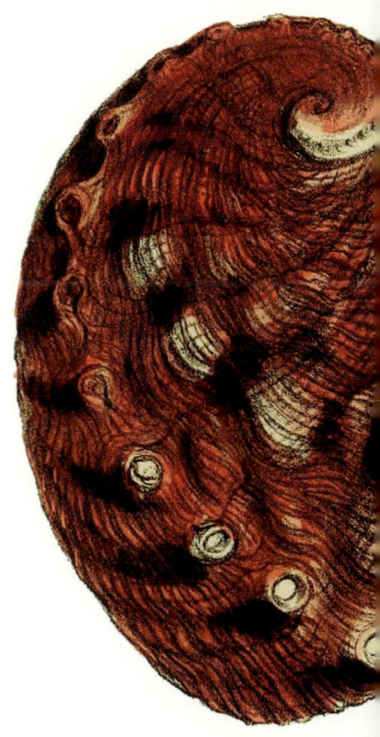

4

Common Limpet

PATELLA VULGATA

CLASS
Gastropoda

RANGE
Atlantic

HABITAT
Rocky shorelines to
depths of 2 m (6½ ft)

SIZE
6 cm (2½ in) across

OF NOTE
Homing behaviour; radula
is tougher than steel

DISCOVER MORE

At the shore, limpet shells can look like numerous party hats dotting the rocky outcrops. That classic shape – the broad base and hydrodynamic cone – are the ideal form to minimise the drag from waves.

There's more to the limpet's cling than just shape, though. Try to gently move one and you'll feel the resistance increase in response. A limpet can cling so strongly that its shell will usually break before it releases its grip. It was once thought that a limpet created a vacuum under its foot, but calculations showed that suction couldn't account for the powerful cling. The answer, scientists recently discovered, is a different kind of trick in its foot. It releases an adhesive mucus that acts like a temporary glue.

If you find a tide pool where you can watch a submerged limpet, you might see it peek out from under its shell. Its head has two tentacles that it uses for sniffing around for a meal of seaweed. At the base of each tentacle is an eyespot, which allows the snail to see light, dark, and maybe some shadows, but not any crisp images. There's also a mouth, inside of which is the mollusk's toothy tongue, called a radula.

The limpet's radula is one of the most extraordinary biological structures known. Formed from iron nanofibers embedded in a special protein, the material is thirteen times stronger than steel, capable of withstanding forces between 3 and 6.5 GPa. Imagine 500,000 pounds (1.1 million kg) in 1 square inch (2.5 cm²)! It's a record holder for strength, outperforming spider silk (often considered the strongest natural material). We humans haven't even been able to build materials much stronger than the humble limpet's radula.

Watch a limpet a little longer. You might see it wander off to graze. Left behind on the rock is an indentation or "home scar" cut into the stony surface—a perfect imprint of the animal's shell. Just before the tide returns, the limpet will follow the scent of its mucus back to this exact spot—a behavior called homing. It will fit its shell precisely in place, and ready itself for whatever swells the sea sends its way.

5

Pelican Foot

APORRHAIS PESPELECANI

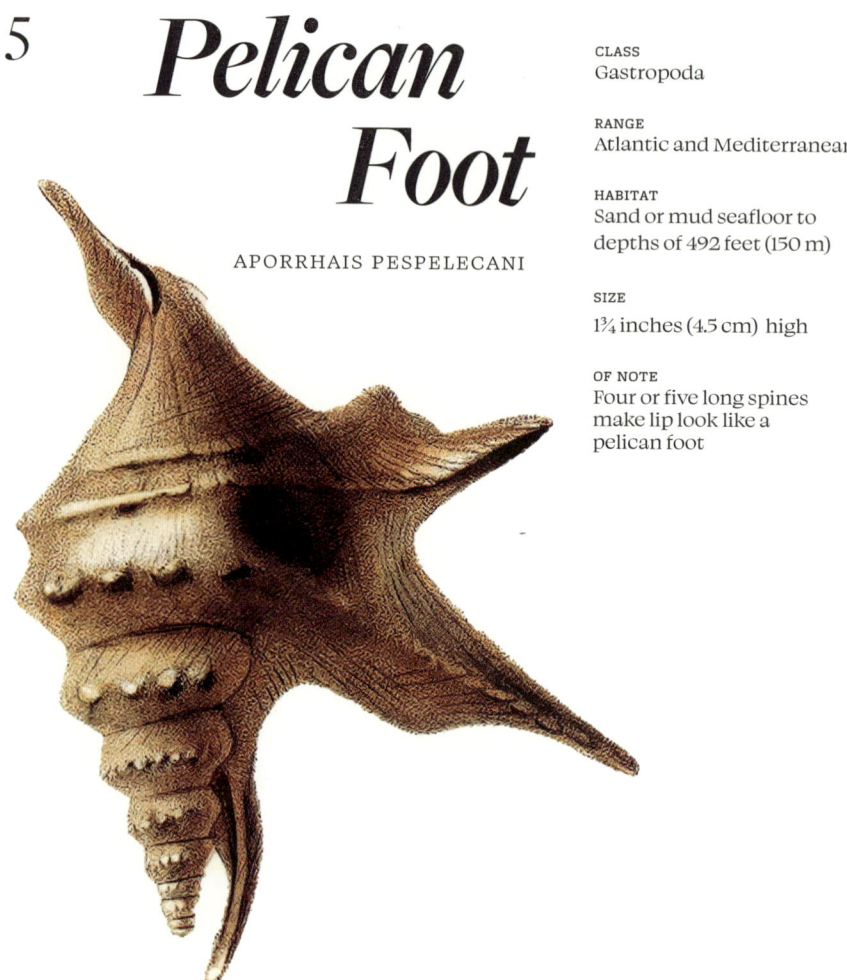

CLASS
Gastropoda

RANGE
Atlantic and Mediterranean

HABITAT
Sand or mud seafloor to depths of 492 feet (150 m)

SIZE
1¾ inches (4.5 cm) high

OF NOTE
Four or five long spines make lip look like a pelican foot

DISCOVER MORE

Glance at the pelican foot and you can see why the animal has its name. Its shell's outer lip has four or five webbed extensions that look convincingly like the foot of the grand seabird. The pelican foot's close cousins are tropical conchs, like the queen conch, which has a similarly fabulous flair.

In 1936, celebrated marine biologist Sir Charles Maurice Yonge described the pelican foot snail's awkward jump. The foot remaining motionless, the body and the shell are carried forward in one convulsive movement. Such ungainliness is probably because a pelican foot snail isn't at home on a flat surface.

Place a pelican foot on a bed of sandy gravel, Yonge writes, and all of a sudden, its unusual extensions make sense. It lives to bury. Think of how your outstretched fingers can easily tunnel into wet sand.

Starting with the smallest extension at the shell's end, the snail pushes beneath the surface, first downward and then horizontally. Each time it moves, the animal shifts a little to the right, digging its side-directed extensions deeper. A hill of gravel forms on top of the shell, and as the snail keeps moving down, forward, and to the right, grains tumble down, covering the back of the spiral.

Once fully submerged, the animal's proboscis—a long, flexible, nose-like structure—reaches past the shell's littlest digit until it breaks the sand's surface. It excavates a circular hole, $\frac{1}{16}$ inch (2 mm) in diameter, while at the same time consolidating the sand grains with mucus. Now, the snail can inhale water as if through a sand snorkel. Initial construction job completed, the snail withdraws its proboscis and begins to build a second tube on the far side of the shell—this one for exhalation. Once that's built, the snail remains in its cozy burrow for up to three days, filtering plankton from the water for food.

This system is a lot like a clam's, which also buries itself but has two siphons: one for inhaling and one for exhaling. The pelican's foot manages to create a similar setup with just one proboscis. Couple its clam-like lifestyle with the extraordinary extensions of its shell and, as Yonge concludes, this snail is "unique amongst the Gastropoda."

6

Greater Argonaut

ARGONAUTA ARGO

CLASS
Cephalopoda

RANGE
Tropical and temperate
waters worldwide

HABITAT
Open ocean

SIZE
Up to 12 inches (30 cm)

OF NOTE
Shell is actually a modified
egg case and can be repaired

DISCOVER MORE

Almost 200 years ago, a French-born dressmaker named Jeanne Villepreux-Power placed a lifetime of work on a ship bound for England. She would follow by land from Sicily where she and her husband, an English merchant, had been living for years.

In Sicily, Villepreux-Power had become fascinated with the sea. Drawing on her knowledge of design, she built the first known aquaria to better observe ocean animals. Among the many marine mysteries she solved was that of the argonaut shell, a delicate, white spiral with elegant ridges and knobs. The English word argonaut means sailor of the ship *Argo*, which the legendary Jason sailed with the help of the divine in order to find the Golden Fleece.

The argonaut shell has been a subject of fascination and debate for centuries. Because of its fragility, finding an argonaut shell on the shore has always been a rare event. But when a fisherperson pulls up one in a net, it isn't a snail or a clam but an octopus living inside. Was an octopus capable of making a shell? In the fourth century BCE, Aristotle declared it impossible and said the cephalopod stole the shell, like a hermit crab. But, if so, from whom?

Villepreux-Power collected argonaut eggs and watched baby octopuses hatch in her aquaria. At birth, they had no shells. But as female octopuses matured, they began secreting the material from their two front arms that eventually formed an argonaut shell. Villepreux-Power discovered the shell was a case for holding eggs, and a female could deposit up to 170,000 inside.

All this research, and more, was packed onto the ship, so Villepreux-Power could publish and present her findings to academics in London at a time when women were considered incapable of doing science. Then, tragedy struck. The ship hit a terrible storm and sank.

Determined not to let her efforts succumb to the ocean, Villepreux-Power returned to Sicily and repeated her observations, precisely documenting everything again. Like a hermit crab, one male scientist tried to steal her discovery. But like the argonaut, Villepreux-Power ultimately received credit for the work she generated herself.

7

CLASS
Cephalopoda

RANGE
Australia to Micronesia

HABITAT
Open ocean

SIZE
Up to 10 inches (25 cm)

OF NOTE
Growth follows a nearly
perfect logarithmic spiral

Chambered Nautilus

NAUTILUS POMPILIUS

DISCOVER MORE

Around 300 million years ago, the clans to which squid and octopus belong discovered that being flexible had great advantages for swimming and dispensed with cumbersome shells, but not the nautiluses. They held fast to ancient ways and today are the only cephalopods that still build shells.

What incredible shells they are. Like zebras, each nautilus shell has unique stripes. The colors range from orange and brown to purple. The top is slightly darker than the bottom— an evolutionary technique called countershading, which helps the animals blend with the sea's changing light.

Nautilus shells are lined in pearlescent nacre and sectioned into compartments. A baby nautilus starts off with just four, and lives in the closest chamber to the opening. As it grows, it builds a bigger chamber, seals off the previous one, and moves into the larger space. At 15 years, it may have as many as forty chambers.

The inner chambers are used for buoyancy, filling with water for sinking or gas for rising, and a jet of water expelled through a siphon moves the animal to and fro. That siphon is surrounded by up to ninety grooved tentacles coated in a sticky secretion for grasping food.

Cut in two, the elegant nautilus shell is often cited as an example of the "golden spiral," but in 1999, a mathematician spent a week at the California Academy of Sciences measuring archived nautilus shells, and debunked the age-old claim. He found that the shells' size increases by a constant ratio on each rotation, making their swirl perfectly logarithmic, but the ratio varies from 1.24 to 1.43, not the golden ratio of approximately 1.616.

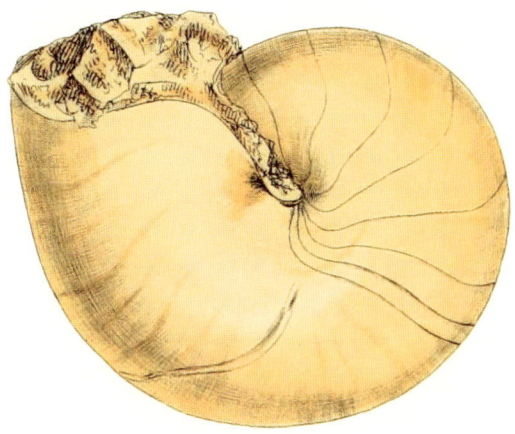

8

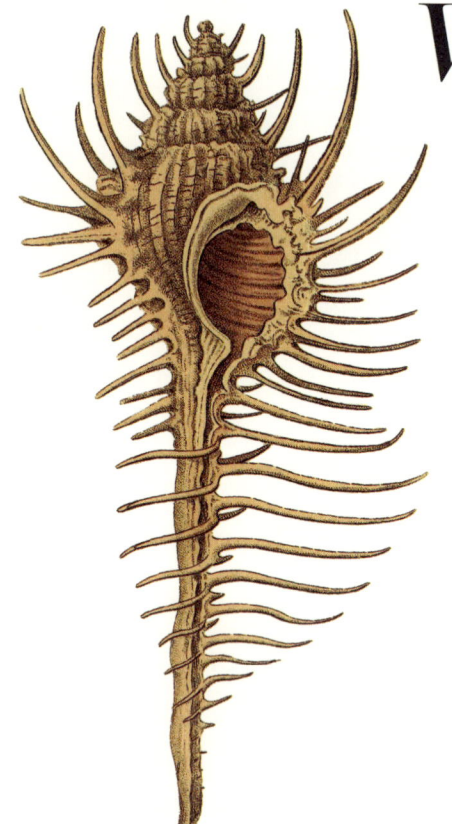

Venus Comb

MUREX PECTEN

CLASS
Gastropoda

RANGE
Indo-Pacific

HABITAT
Sand or mud seafloor to
depths of 984 feet (300 m)

SIZE
Up to 6 inches (15 cm)

OF NOTE
Long, striking spines
form a protective cage
around the animal

DISCOVER MORE

This stunning snail, found in the tropical waters off Indonesia and the Philippines, is cream to brownish with pale banding. What makes it so unusual are the more than 100 long, sharp spines that adorn its shell from tip to tail. These are hollow inside, formed by a buckling of the mantle. A long siphon adds to the shell's undeniable drama.

The elaborate spines likely have a few different purposes. They act as buoys, preventing the snail from sinking into soft, muddy seafloors, and they come in handy as protection and maybe even for capturing food. The spines extending off either side of the shell form a cage around the vulnerable, soft body, and the third row points straight upward, making it look a bit like a knight in prickly armor. It is also thought that the cage of spines might trap small crabs and worms inside with the snail, helping it to capture prey.

Like others in the *Murex* clan, the Venus comb is a carnivore, hunting alone at night for clams and other small mollusks. It releases a fluid to soften the prey's shell and then scrapes away at the weakened area with its radula.

Unlike other gastropods, the Venus comb snail moves with its long siphon in the front. Like a forward-facing nose, the siphon draws in water, which washes over its gills and chemical receptors, giving the animal information about the surrounding seas. Despite its abundant armor, the Venus comb does have its predators. It's eaten by fish, stingrays, and sharks, as well as humans.

The Venus comb's name, though poetic, has a fuzzy origin story. It's probably connected to the famous image of Venus by Renaissance painter Botticelli. Venus's maid holds a shell in her hand as if to comb Venus's hair, but it looks a lot more like a mussel shell than a Venus comb. Some specimens of the same shell were called by the much less charming name "thorny woodcock," maybe because the long siphonal canal looks like the long, thin beak of that bird. When scientists later determined that the two names actually described the same species, the Venus comb, thankfully, won out.

9

Lightning Whelk

SINISTROFULGUR
PERVERSUM

CLASS
Gastropoda

RANGE
New Jersey to Mexico

HABITAT
Sand or mud seafloor to
depths of 150 feet (45 m)

SIZE
2½–16 inches (6–40 cm)

OF NOTE
Left-handed spiral

DISCOVER MORE

The lightning whelk is, in most
respects, classic looking. Its shell is a
tan color with darker brown lightning
stripes from top to bottom and a
steep shoulder with short spines. Its
aperture is pear-shaped. The snail's
body is dark brown or black.

Lightning whelks build an egg case,
which is sometimes called a mermaid's
necklace, 11–33 inches (27–83 cm) in
length. It's a chain of as many as 145
capsules, each holding several
developing eggs. Only about a dozen
will hatch, and the snail's predatory
behavior begins right away when the
first hatchlings will eat the unhatched
eggs. Once it grows into an adult, the
animal seeks out bivalves to eat by
smelling for them under the mud.
Then it slips its shell inside the opening
between shells and waits for the prey to
tire. As its shell needs to withstand the
clam's clamp without breaking, its
density is extremely robust.

When you look at lightning whelk shells from the top, the differences from your average whelk become apparent. Rather than coil in a clockwise direction, like nearly every other shell, its spiral is counterclockwise. This puts its aperture on the left when facing you, making it left-handed or sinistral.

The lightning whelk's genus name, *Sinistrofulgur* couples the Latin-rooted word for "left" and also "menacing" with the word "fulgur," meaning lightning. For good measure, its second name is based on the word "perverse," meaning "turning away from the right." The taxonomists don't want you to forget this shell is different.

Native Americans didn't see the shell's spin as sinister or perverse. Archaeologists suggest that the Calusa, who lived in what is now Southwest Florida between 500 and 1700 CE, imbued the shell with particular spiritual value. They are thought to have viewed the shell's counterclockwise spiral in alignment with the movement of the sun, from right to left when facing north. A caffeinated ritual beverage called "black drink" made with yaupon holly was served in large lighting whelk shells. The drink kept people awake during ceremonies involving vision quests, which could last for days. The Calusa also used the shell to make axes, spearpoints, containers, and jewelry. Hundreds of lightning whelks (or a similar-looking extinct relation also called a lightning whelk, *Busycon perversum*) in burial sites as far inland as Kentucky are a testament to this unusual shell's value.

10 *Horse Conch*

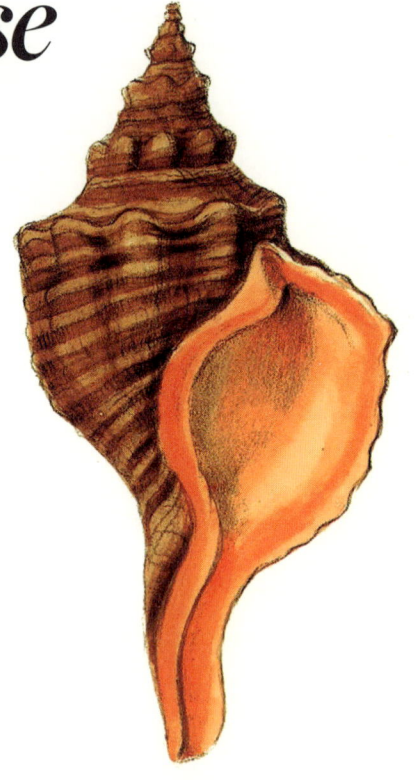

TRIPLOFUSUS
GIGANTEUS

CLASS
Gastropoda

RANGE
North Carolina to Mexico

HABITAT
Sand or mud seafloor to
depths of 656 feet (200 m)

SIZE
Up to 2 feet (66 cm)

OF NOTE
The biggest snail
in North America

DISCOVER MORE

The horse conch's claim to fame comes from being the biggest snail in North America, second only to the Australian trumpet (*Syrinx aruanus*) globally. It can weigh as much as 11 pounds (5 kg) and reach a whopping 2 feet (66 cm).

Technically, the horse conch is not a conch. It's a member of the family that includes tulip and spindle snails, called Fasciolariidae, rather than the conchs, which are members of Strombidae. Its common name seems to have stuck, and now that it is the state shell of Florida, there's likely no going back.

The horse conch's shell is sculpted with axial ribs and chords along the whorls. In places, this results in prominent knobs. The shell has a pointed spire and a rather large, pear-shaped aperture with a visible siphonal canal.

When the horse conch is young its shell is orange, but as it ages the shell turns salmon and then gray. Because it's so massive, the snail moves slowly, and often becomes home to barnacles, worms, and other encrusting creatures, making each shell a unique consortium of life.

As a predator, the horse conch smothers its prey with its massive bright reddish-orange foot. It probably also releases some toxins to help sedate the lightning whelks and tulip snails, razor clams, and crabs that it eats. Although sometimes eaten by sharks and octopuses, the horse conch is considered a top predator, critical to ecosystems because it keeps other populations in check.

Given its conspicuous giant shell, people have a long history with the horse conch. Along with the queen conch (*Strombus gigas*), the Maya carved the shell into trumpets at both coastal and inland sites. Indigenous people from throughout North America prized the snail for its meat and used the shell for drinking vessels, fishing weights, and tools.

This long history with humans comes at a price. In 2022, scientists studied the layers of horse conch shells to look at their age and growth rates, similar to studying tree rings. They discovered that rather than living for many decades as previously thought, even the biggest horse conchs are probably just teenagers. An average horse conch only lives about 8 to 10 years and reaches maturity at 6. This gives the snail just a few years to reproduce and makes the animals extremely vulnerable to overharvesting. So, if you are lucky enough to see a live horse conch, be sure to leave it in the sea.

11

Scotch Bonnet

SEMICASSIS GRANULATA

CLASS
Gastropoda

RANGE
North Carolina to Uruguay

HABITAT
Sand or mud seafloor to depths of 656 feet (200 m)

SIZE
2–4 inches (5–10 cm)

OF NOTE
Builds an egg tower that looks similar to the Tower of Pisa's architecture

DISCOVER MORE

Some say that the Scotch bonnet got its name because it looks like a classic Scottish Tam O'shanter hat. Indeed, its compact shell with brown to yellow crisscrosses looks like a passable plaid. The thick outer lip with deep grooves resembles the brim of a cap, completing the look of a bonnet.

Once that thick lip forms, the snail stops growing for a while. Then, when it's ready to grow again, it absorbs the thick lip until it reaches its new size, whereupon it grows a new lip. Once in a while, the lip won't absorb all the way and is incorporated into the shell—a rare feature known as a varix.

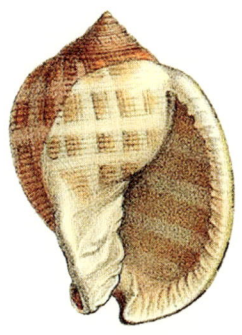

Intricacy is part of this animal's brand. When the female is ready to lay her eggs, she constructs a complicated structure that looks like a 5 inch- (13 cm-) tall Tower of Pisa. The male then fertilizes the eggs in the tower and when they are ready to hatch, tiny veliger larvae emerge. They swim in the oceans for up to 14 weeks, before returning to the seafloor.

Scotch bonnet snails are predatory, feeding on sand dollars and sea biscuits. They dissolve echinoderms' outer skeletons by releasing a serum of sulfuric acid.

So much consternation has surrounded its taxonomy that the Scotch bonnet has had thirty-eight different scientific names. There's a similar-looking snail from the Mediterranean and eastern North Atlantic, *Semicassis undulata*, though its plaid is a richer ocher. It is currently considered a separate species, although in the past the two have been merged.

In 1965, in honor of the contributions of the Scottish population who had immigrated to their state, the members of a shell club in North Carolina proposed making the Scotch bonnet their state shell. It would be the first such designation in the US, but convincing the North Carolina State Congress wasn't easy. To impress upon his fellow legislators the value of passing a law about seashells, the proposing state representative promised a keepsake shell to all legislators who supported him. Many were initially willing, but when the legislator was able to find only two Scotch bonnets, his colleagues grew hesitant. The law passed and a collector made sure that each of the 170 representatives were given the Scotch bonnet they were due.

12

Shark Eye

NEVERITA DUPLICATA

CLASS
Gastropoda

RANGE
Massachusetts to Honduras

HABITAT
Sand or mud seafloor to
depths of 164 feet (50 m)

SIZE
Up to 3½ inches (9 cm)

OF NOTE
Has a distinctive collar-
shaped egg case

DISCOVER MORE

Walking over a sand bar on the US east coast when the tide's just going out, there's a good chance you'll see a trail in the sand about 1 inch (2.5 cm) wide. If you follow the trail to its end, you'll find a mound of sand, and peeking out like an eye staring up from the beach itself will be a snail about the size of a ping-pong ball. The smooth, rounded, low-spired shell has a darker center whorl that gives it an ocular look and its moniker: shark eye. Sometimes the shell will have a blue color in the center, in which case it's called a Paul Newman for the actor's famous eye color.

Dip your hand underneath the sand mound and you'll find yourself cradling an astonishingly large snail for its shell size. Its beige foot can extend to three times the diameter of the shell because when it's out hunting, it inflates its body with water. When startled, the snail expels the water, retreats inside its shell, and closes itself inside with a soft operculum.

If you are very quick indeed (and even better if you're a child), gently place the pad of your finger on the bottom of the snail's foot. It will grip your finger as it contracts, creating a fabulous press-on "finger-snail." Just be sure to take off your mollusk manicure after a minute or two and carefully return the animal to its home.

Shark eyes belong to a large family of predatory gastropods called moon snails, which are found all over the world.

In 1931, malacologist Julia E. Rogers wrote vividly of the animal's hunting behavior:

> This blind, mole-like mollusk finds plenty to eat in the zone just under the surface of the sand. Clams and other shell fish are there. Down comes the hood from over the head when a victim is met. The long proboscis is set, and the radula it contains soon has a neat round hole drilled in the shell, through which the soft parts are extracted by the sucking mouth of the bloodthirsty [moon snail].

In summer, you might come across something that looks like it's made of a translucent plastic with the form and thickness of a large orange peel. These are called sand collars and are egg cases made from mucus and sand by mother shark eyes. Once the baby snails hatch, the collars become fragile and dissolve.

13

Bay Scallop

ARGOPECTAN IRRADIANS

CLASS
Bivalva

RANGE
Massachusetts to Texas

HABITAT
Seagrass meadows to
depths of 60 feet (18 m)

SIZE
Up to 3½ inches (9 cm)

OF NOTE
Has eighteen to forty
bright-blue eyes

DISCOVER MORE

If you get the chance to look at a bay scallop, be aware it's looking back at you. Along the edge of its shell are many small eyes, each one robin's egg blue and outfitted with a lens, retina, cornea, and optic nerve, allowing the scallop to see you tilting your head to consider just why a bivalve needs so much optical capacity. It's because, unlike most sedentary bivalves, bay scallops are mobile, and they need eyes to see when to move.

Bay scallops have two shells, the upper one a little darker and mottled, the lower one white. The shells are ribbed, and near the hinge are a pair of winglike ears, with one slightly smaller. Unlike other bivalves, the bay scallop doesn't have a siphon and its foot isn't functional. Instead, it uses a strong adductor muscle to slam shut with such force that it pushes a jet of water out from between its shells. This lifts the scallop off the seafloor, allowing it to swim very quickly for short distances.

Because they contain both male and female reproductive organs, bay scallops put a lot of energy into reproduction. Each scallop releases as many as 16 million eggs at a time. That exertion depletes them, and they usually spawn just once in their lifetime, which lasts about 18 months.

Once fertilized, a scallop larva turns into a D-shaped veliger complete with two tiny shells. It swims through the ocean for as long as 2 weeks. During that time, it develops into a mini scallop called a spat. The spat hopefully finds a welcoming patch of a type of seagrass called eelgrass, extrudes tiny silky threads called byssal, and grabs on tight. After 2–6 weeks of hanging onto the eelgrass, the spat morphs again into a tiny scallop, releases its hold, and falls to the seafloor. There it lives out the rest of its life, jetting about now and then to escape predation.

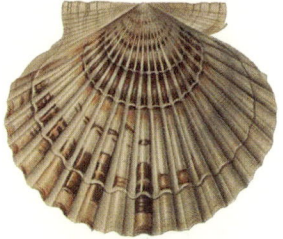

Once a significant fishery along the east coast of the United States, as seagrass beds declined due to coastal development and pollution, so too have the bay scallops. In Maryland's Chesapeake Bay, authorities planted 1.2 million baby bay scallops in an attempt to bring back populations. A few years later, bay scallops returned to estuaries where they hadn't been seen for more than a century. Their populations are still at risk, so any live bay scallops caught should be returned to the sea.

14 *Alphabet Cone*

CONUS SPURIUS

CLASS
Gastropod

RANGE
Florida to Venezuela

HABITAT
Coral reefs to depths
of 200 feet (64 m)

SIZE
Up to 3¼ inches (8 cm)

OF NOTE
The shell's markings look
like letters

DISCOVER MORE

When you're looking for shells on the beach, it's easy to imagine secret messages in what you find. Nothing brings out that feeling more than the alphabet cone. It's palm-sized with a steep shoulder and low spire. Its background is white with a pattern of orange-, dun-, or chocolate-colored markings, which make it a subject of wonder. The distinctive spots and dashes look like the markings in ancient clay tablets or letters.

In the shelling hotspot of Sanibel Island, Florida, shell collectors treasure these gastropod shells, which wash up with some regularity. One local couple has found every single letter on the alphabet cones they've discovered. Self-titled "shellebrity" Pam Rambo, who has covered her entire VW Beetle in a mosaic of shells, posted a single alphabet cone that spelled three words: pie, kit, and six. Its meaning remains for the beholder to interpret.

Like other cone snails, the alphabet snail is a predator. It injects toxins with a spear-like radula to subdue its prey, which includes clams and other bivalves. If a person gets caught in its trajectory, its sting is likened to that of a bee. Before picking up an alphabet cone, double-check to make sure no animal is inside.

If you find a shard of alphabet cone, there's an interesting story to read in it as well. You might notice that the inner spiral and whorl layers have regions that look hollow. That's because the snail dissolves parts of its shell to make space for its body. When it swallows large prey, it has room to expand into the available space. The snail can also recycle parts of that internal shell to thicken the outer walls, building a better defense against predators.

While the alphabet cone only lives in the Atlantic, it has a Pacific counterpart. The lettered cone snail, *Conus litteratus*, flaunts slightly darker markings. It ranges from Madagascar in the east to Australia in the west and from the Philippines in the south to Japan in the north. Anthropologists have found bracelets made of lettered cone shells in the graves of the elite class of women of the Yayoi people of Japan's Kyushu Island. As early as 300 BCE, Yayoi sailors braved treacherous journeys as far as Korea and Okinawa in search of these fascinating shells, their cryptic messages just as captivating centuries ago as they are now.

15

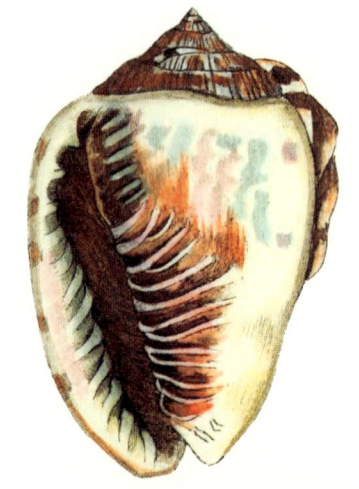

Queen Helmet

CASSIS MADAGASCARIENSIS

CLASS
Gastropod

RANGE
Florida to US Virgin Islands

HABITAT
Sand or mud seafloor to
depths of 600 feet (183 m)

SIZE
Up to 14 inches (36 cm)

OF NOTE
Prized in the Victorian era
for cameos

DISCOVER MORE

The largest helmet snail in the Caribbean, queen helmets well represent the armor for which they are named. Their bulky shells are hat-shaped, with impressive spikes surrounding the whorls. The aperture is surrounded by a thick, flattened orange lip (shield) and lined with white teeth. They are a creamy white color, with orange and chestnut markings.

Helmet snails are predators, eating urchins, sand dollars, and sea biscuits.

These gastropods move slowly, pulling their spires behind them. When they come across an echinoderm, they launch their large foot up and over the top, bringing their shell with them. The whole animal then collapses downward, trapping its prey. To remove the prickly outer layer of the echinoderm, the snail produces saliva that contains sulfuric acid, which dissolves the echinoderm spines. It then drills a hole in the calcium carbonate shell, releasing more secretions that anesthetize its prey.

Queen helmet names are somewhat puzzling. The animal is sometimes called Clench's helmet or Emperor helmet. And while the king helmet snail (*Cassis tuberosa*) is also a Caribbean species, the queen helmet is larger. (Besides size, one way to tell the two apart is that the king helmet's outer lip has dark brown triangular bars, but the queen helmet's does not.)

Also perplexing is its scientific name, which means "of Madagascar," although Madagascar is halfway around the world from the queen helmet's habitat in the Caribbean. As a medium for jewelry, the queen helmet shell is sometimes called sardonyx, another name for agate rocks.

This last designation may help explain some of the confusion, which likely has its origin during the sixteenth and seventeenth centuries, when conchylomania was at its height. Ships returned to Europe with a variety of shells from around the world. This was also a time when cameos—jewelry made from carvings in relief, usually with a different color background—were extremely popular. Some were made from gem-quality rocks, like orange carnelian, green jade, or banded agate, but supply was low and cost high.

Shells offered an alternative. Of particular advantage, queen helmet shells naturally change colors when carved: the surface layers are lighter and the deeper layers darker, making for a stunning canvas for artists carving cameos. At a time when shells were entering the market from the Indo-Pacific, it's possible that the Caribbean's queen helmet was misnamed as "from Madagascar" to inflate its price when it was carved into jewelry.

16

Precious Wentletrap

EPITONIUM SCALARE

CLASS
Gastropoda

RANGE
Tropical Indo-Pacific

HABITAT
Coral reefs and sandy
seafloor

SIZE
1–2¾ inches (2.5–7 cm)

OF NOTE
Fakes were once made
from rice

DISCOVER MORE

If you've got a soft spot for tiny, beautiful shells, be on the lookout for wentletraps. Usually, they aren't much bigger than a couple of centimeters. They are pearly or whitish with a steep spire and elegant ribbing—technically called costae—that runs vertically down the whorls, which are not fused together. This gives the shell the appearance of having circular banisters running along its length and led to the wentletrap name, which translates to "spiral staircase" in Dutch. In English, they are also known as staircase shells.

While those ridges give the shells a whimsical look that could have inspired drawings of the turrets of fairytale castles, they do more than add to the architectural beauty of the shells. The costae probably act as obstructions to predators that might want to drill a hole in the shell, preventing them from clamping down.

Wentletrap snails belong to the expansive family Epitoniidae, which includes more than 50 genera and 650 species. The group has undergone numerous reorganizations since the advent of DNA sequencing. In 2017, violet snails in the genus *Janthina*, which live their entire lives floating on the ocean's surface, moved into the wentletrap clan.

Although *Janthina*'s shell doesn't have the characteristic steep spire and ribbing like the classic wentletraps, it also makes a purple-colored anesthetic, which is used to relax and immobilize its prey. Found in all oceans, from the Arctic to the Antarctic, wentletraps often live near sea anemones and coral, which are their favorite foods. They lay their eggs in capsules that become covered in sand and look much like discarded beaded necklaces.

The English name "precious" is apt because during the Renaissance this shell fetched hefty prices. One of the first shell chroniclers, the Dutch collector Rumphius, was forced to sell his precious wentletrap to Cosimo III de Medici, the Grand Duke of Tuscany, when only three specimens were known to exist in Europe. Later, Rumphius tried to buy one back for about $6,500 in today's money, but his offer wasn't high enough. The first four specimens arrived in London in 1743 and sold at auction for the equivalent of $14,000. European rulers, including the Queen of Sweden and Catherine the Great, also amassed the tiny treasures. At one point, demand was so great that craftspeople in China modeled fakes from rice paste to appease Chinese emperors who wanted them. Today, only a few fakes survive and are rarer than the shells they imitated.

17 Banded Wedge Shells

DONAX VITTATUS

CLASS
Bivalvia

RANGE
Eastern Atlantic and
Mediterranean

HABITAT
Sandy seafloor to depths
of 66 feet (20 m)

SIZE
1¼ inches (3.3 cm)

OF NOTE
An important food for birds,
sea stars, and flatfish

DISCOVER MORE

This delicate bivalve is common on sandy beaches throughout northwest Europe. Its paired shells are found in a rainbow of colors—yellow, brown, pink, and violet—and the inside is white, sometimes stained with yellow, orange, or purple. As their name implies, the shells are wedge-shaped and asymmetrical. The longer side is rounded and the shorter side a little more triangular. They are etched with fine lines radiating from the umbo outward as well as concentric bands. Often, you can see annual rings, as on a tree, with a darker band demarcating a new year. The animals usually live for 2 or 3 years, but if conditions are good, they can reach 7 years.

The banded wedge shell has a large foot and two tentacles, one slightly longer than the other. The foot tunnels down into the sand and then expands with blood, which anchors it in place. Then the animal pulls against its foot, bringing the rest of its body down until it is buried. The flattened shell with its angular form helps it slip easily through the sand.

Once buried, the animal extends two siphons up above the sand's surface like periscopes. The longer siphon moves around, searching for food with sensory organs located on its end and sucking in food-filled water like a straw. The clam's gills sort the good food from the waste, which gets puffed out of the shorter siphon like a smokestack spitting out exhaust.

While the animals don't have eyes, they sense light. In experiments, researchers cast a shadow across the sand where the banded wedges were buried. They quickly moved a little closer to the surface to ensure they wouldn't be buried too deep for their siphons to reach the seafloor. When the researchers removed the shadow, the animals returned to their previous location a little deeper.

Underwater videos show banded wedge shells are most active around low tide, when the water is most disturbed and more food to eat floats around. This is also when the bivalves run the risk of being unearthed by scouring waves. If that happens, the animal is described as "leaping" to quickly rebury itself. That's because gulls, sea stars, snails, flounders, and plaice are all on the hunt at low tide and banded wedge shells are on their menu. A study from the Scottish coast found that as many as 18 percent of banded wedge bivalves showed signs of siphon damage from nips by predators. They also discovered that the wounds healed quickly. Within 10 days, the animals entirely regenerated.

18

Painted Top-snail

CALLIOSTOMA ZIZYPHINUM

CLASS
Gastropoda

RANGE
Atlantic and Mediterranean

HABITAT
Rocky shoreline to depths
of 300 feet (50 m)

SIZE
1¼ inches (3.3 cm)

OF NOTE
Looks like a child's toy,
named for Sisyphus

DISCOVER MORE

Painted top-snails are common on the rocky shores from Norway to the Azores. As an adult, its shell has twelve to thirteen whorls, each with four tiny ridges that look like they are made from tiny beads. Its color can be tan, yellow, brown, pale pink, or violet with streaks and blotches of brown, red, or purple at the edges. Painted top-snails graze algae. They have two tentacles on either side of their head and four more on each side of their body. About a thousand species of top-snails exist, which share a similarly conical-shaped shell that looks like an upside-down toy top.

Carl Linnaeus, who was the eighteenth century's great namer of animals, dubbed the species *zizyphinum*, which has been the subject of much debate. Some connected it to the mottled colors of the *Ziziphus jujube* plant, others with the Greek myth of Sisyphus.

If you happen upon a top-snail, consider its cone-like shape, and what you make of this tale of Sisyphus.

As king of ancient Corinth, Sisyphus was hoping for a new spring for his city. At the same time, the river god Asopus was looking for his daughter, who was hiding from him. Sisyphus located Asopus's daughter and traded the information for new waterworks, but Zeus didn't want her found and Sisyphus betrayed Zeus when he divulged the truth.

To avenge the betrayal, Zeus sent Thanatos (the personification of death) to find Sisyphus and chain him in a deep dungeon. The quick-tongued Sisyphus asked Thanatos to demonstrate how the chains worked, and in the process entrapped Thanatos. Thus trapped, no one could die on earth, which was so problematic that Ares, the god of war, had to intervene. For being difficult, the gods devised a punishment for Sisyphus that would teach him, over and over, what it means to think you can outsmart death. The ex-king was forced to roll a boulder up a steep hill. Just before it reached the top, the boulder would roll down again, for eternity.

With the Latin name of this shell, Linnaeus might have wanted to draw attention to its inclined sides, reflective of the mountain on which Sisyphus was condemned to labor, but there's more to the story than constant defeat. Some scholars interpret the story as resembling the rising and setting of the sun, or the rising and falling of the waves. French writer Camus suggested that the myth's lesson is that the journey is what really matters: "The struggle itself toward the heights is enough to fill a man's heart."

NATURE'S MASTERPIECES: THIRTY SHELLS

19

Common Periwinkle

LITTORINA LITTOREA

CLASS
Gastropoda

RANGE
North Carolina to Siberia

HABITAT
Rocky shoreline to depths
of 196 feet (60 m)

SIZE
Up to 1¼ inches (3 cm)

OF NOTE
Sold by street vendors
called winkle men

DISCOVER MORE

These little snails are familiar to most people who've strolled rocky shorelines on both sides of the Atlantic. They are marble-sized and colored purple, gray, or blue, with a white inner lip. You might be fooled when you pick one up and find long legs popping out of the bottom. The shells are favorites of hermit crabs.

Periwinkles live in the zone between low and high tide, grazing the rocks for algae and the eggs of other mollusks, and hiding out in tide pools in crevasses when the tide ebbs. Sometimes they get caught out on the bare rocks, which makes them susceptible to drying out, so they have developed a hard operculum that they can use to seal themselves inside their shell. A low tide gives periwinkles a reprieve from predators such as dogwhelks, crabs, and sea stars, but it also exposes them to attacks from seabirds and us.

Humans have had a long history with periwinkles. In Europe, archaeological remains suggest that almost 10,000 years ago people used them for food and to dye their clothing a bluish purple. While the need for periwinkle dyes faded over the centuries, the taste for the snails grew.

By the 1800s in England, public houses and eateries sold periwinkles to enjoy with a cup of tea. Winkle men sold snails out of baskets or barrels, boiled then salted, often with a pin to pick out the meat. As one of the cheapest forms of protein, a shopper could buy enough for a hearty snack for just half a penny.

On the other side of the Atlantic, periwinkles were first noted in Canada in 1841 and quickly spread as far south as Delaware. Today, their numbers can reach as high as 700 per square yard (about a square meter). Diners in the Americas never developed a taste for periwinkles, but they did establish a lucrative fishery. Tons were shipped back to England to fill winkle shops.

Scientists have debated how periwinkles made it to the Americas. Most thought they were brought by the English who wanted a familiar food in the 1800s. The snails were considered a classic example of a human-mediated invasive species. But in 2008, genetic studies showed that American periwinkle DNA differed from that of European periwinkles, and that the populations separated about 20,000 years ago, well before the advent of winkle shops. This suggests the snails rode out the last ice age somewhere in Nova Scotia and made their way south as shipping increased.

20

Common Piddock

PHOLAS DACTYLUS

CLASS
Bivalvia

RANGE
Brazil to Greenland,
UK to Turkey

HABITAT
Rocky shoreline to depths
of 115 feet (35 m)

SIZE
Up to 5 inches (13 cm)

OF NOTE
The sorcerer behind
the holes in hagstones

DISCOVER MORE

Perhaps you've walked along a beach and seen stones with perfect cylinders, 1 inch (2.5 cm) or so in width, drilled right through them. In England, some people call these rocks hagstones or witch stones because they believe them to have magical powers. Sailors used to thread a rope through the holes and hang the rocks off the sides of their ships to keep away bad weather.

Farmers hung them in their stables to protect their horses. Some wore them around their necks in order to ward off evil spirits.

Those holes aren't sorcery; they're the work of a clam-like bivalve called the common piddock. Its shells are up to 1 foot (30 cm) long, whitish or pale gray, with concentric ridges and radiating lines. The shape of the shell is similar to a seagull's wing.

A juvenile piddock finds a small indentation in a rock and burrows in. It grips the stone using the suction of its foot and then uses the hard edges of its shell like a file, rocking back and forth, slowly grinding it away. The animal also spins as it bores, making a perfect circle. The hole enlarges and deepens as the animal grows, but it is locked into the stone for life. It eats by extending its two siphons from the top and filtering seawater for plankton.

Some may think that the piddocks are enchanted as their edges glow blue-green. This luminous ability has been known since ancient times, as recorded by both Pliny the Elder and Hippolytus of Rome. Pliny wrote that people's mouths would glow blue when eating the shellfish raw. Hippolytus recounted that pagans used the shellfish as a trick.

More recently, piddocks have bored their way into the medical field. White blood cells are among our first defenses against infection. When these cells detect harmful bacteria, they release chemicals called free radicals, which can damage bacterial cell membranes. The white blood cells, in effect, "know" when someone is sick before symptoms occur. Researchers discovered that the bioluminescent protein that gives piddocks their glow shines when it comes into contact with free radicals. The amount of light produced can tell doctors that someone's immune system is gearing up for a fight, even before the person feels sick. This could help diagnose autoimmune diseases and also help test if treatments are working. Piddocks, it turns out, do have exceptional—if not magical—powers.

21

Eastern Oyster

CRASSOSTREA VIRGINICA

CLASS
Bivalvia

RANGE
North America

HABITAT
Forms reefs in estuaries

SIZE
Up to 10 inches (25 cm)

OF NOTE
Key habitat for other
species; important food

DISCOVER MORE

In 1608, English Captain John Smith survived a terrible journey west across the Atlantic. Landing in the nascent American colonies, he decided to look for a passage to the other side of the continent—and gold if he could find it. He and a few brave sailors traveled into Chesapeake Bay, where they encountered bears, wolves, cougars, and a stingray that almost killed Smith. Smith also recorded in his trip log that the oysters "lay thick as stones." The word Chesapeake itself is derived from the Algonquin word meaning "great shellfish bay."

Eastern oysters' range stretches from the Canadian Maritimes, down the east coast of the US and to all the Gulf of Mexico states. A major economic driver as food and, more recently, because of their association with luxury dining and being an aphrodisiac, they have been exported to Puget Sound in Washington and Hawaii, where they are now common in Pearl Harbor.

After the Civil War, when dredges were developed, oyster harvesting became industrialized. The Chesapeake boasted the largest harvest in the world, reaching a peak of 20 million bushels a year in the 1880s. (A bushel is between 100 and 300 oysters, depending on their size.)

By the 1920s, the oyster haul plummeted to a quarter of that. In 2003, it was just a tenth of a percent of the historic high. At the same time, the water quality and ecosystems in Cheseapeake Bay degraded drastically.

The eastern oyster has an oblong, gray shell, corrugated with uneven ridges. Its bottom shell is flatter than the top, and inside the shells are pearly white. The animal feeds by filtering seawater through its gills, straining out the plankton, then pumping out the cleansed water. A single oyster can filter as much as 50 gallons (almost 200 liters) a day, making it crucial to healthy seawater quality. Oysters also form vast reefs, like corals do. Their uneven shell surfaces increase the area for other animals to use for habitat by fifty-fold. Without oyster reefs, the crabs, worms, snails, and the fish that eat invertebrates all struggle to survive.

In 2015, the Chesapeake became the site of a major project to bring back oysters. In some places, new reefs were built, providing baby oysters with a habitat. In others, baby oysters were seeded into the water, so they could settle on old reefs. In just six years, 99 percent of the rehabilitated reefs were declared a success. Water quality improved, fish returned, and oyster harvests are the highest in decades, all demonstrating that restoration of our ocean ecosystems is possible.

Common Violet Snail

JANTHINA JANTHINA

CLASS
Gastropoda

RANGE
Temperate and tropical
oceans worldwide

HABITAT
Open ocean

SIZE
Up to 1½ inches (4 cm)

OF NOTE
Floats upside down
using a life raft of bubbles

DISCOVER MORE

The second-largest surface on our planet is one that we don't think about very often: that which exists between water and air. But there's a whole ecosystem of animals that live their entire lives on this surface. They are known as the neuston, from the Greek word for swimming.

Colonial jellyfish such as Portuguese man-o'-wars (*Physalia* spp.), by-the-wind-sailors (*Velella velella*), and blue buttons (*Porpita* spp.) make floats and sails that allow them to cruise the surface of the oceans. Blue sea dragons (*Glaucus atlanticus*) are gorgeous sea slugs with frilled edges that live their lives hanging on the underside of the sea's surface. They hunt those jellyfish and then reuse their prey's stinging cells, moving the weaponry into their own tissues as a means of defense.

Common violet snails are not to be missed among this neustonic menagerie. These animals live upside down, suspended on the sea's surface by a raft of bubbles that they blow from their own mucus. Each bubble takes about ten seconds to create, and once it's formed it hardens into something like a plastic buoy.

The snail can make tens of bubbles in a row before they pause for a break, and an entire raft will include dozens. It's a tenuous life, though. The snail cannot swim, and so if it loses its grip on its raft, it falls to the seafloor.

Violet snails start off as males and, as they age, they turn female. Fertilized eggs develop inside the female. Rather than being cast into the ocean as larvae, baby violet snails hatch fully formed. They are immediately capable of—and must begin—building their own rafts.

Violet snails can be attacked from the air and sea, but their coloration is a disguise. Their globose shells are stained blue on the bottom, which faces the sky when it's floating upside down. The color blends with the blue sea, making it hard for birds hunting from above to see. The shell's top is whitish or grayish, mimicking the sun's light and making it hard for fish to see when they look up.

Like other gastropods, violet snails produce a purple venom to paralyze their prey. That color might have been the source of a purple dye called *tekhelet*, used by ancient Jewish people to color the ritual clothing of the High Priest and the tapestries of the Holy Tabernacle, and the fringes (*tzitzit*) on the ritual garments that men wore to pray.

Blue Mussel

MYTILUS EDULIS

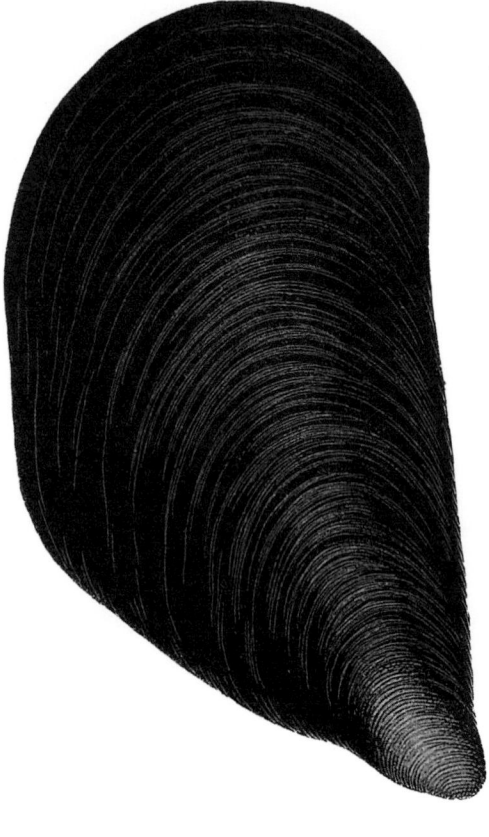

CLASS
Bivalvia

RANGE
Arctic and temperate
North Atlantic

HABITAT
Attached to hard surfaces to
depths of 33 feet (10 m)

SIZE
Up to 8 inches (20 cm)

OF NOTE
Byssus threads are like ropes
on a tent, holding it in place

DISCOVER MORE

The blue mussel is considered a species complex comprised of four different mussel taxa that humans have had a hand in globalizing. *Mytilus edulis* is native to the North Atlantic, but it easily hybridizes with mussels from the Mediterranean, Chile, New Zealand, and the North Pacific. These mussels can withstand a huge range of environments, including freezing conditions for several months and water only half as salty as normal seawater. That incredible range of tolerance is why blue mussels' tight clusters of dark blue, almost black shells are iconic garlands on the legs of piers throughout the world.

Unlike oysters, which cement themselves to surfaces, mussels secure themselves with threads called byssus. Their foot has a gland which produces a thick, glue-like substance that hardens into a tough cord almost as soon as it's secreted and attaches to a hard surface.

Mussels send threads out in many directions, anchoring them in place no matter which directions the currents pull. Because it's not cemented down, a mussel can swing around like a weathervane if the bed isn't too tightly packed. Sometimes threads break or wear out, and if that happens the mussel might crawl around a little before reattaching. Newer mussels tend to settle on top of old ones, and, to avoid being smothered, mussels vie for position. A mussel bed is a dynamic structure, constantly shifting and readjusting.

Mussel beds are grazed by seabirds, fish, sea stars, sea urchins, and us. A staple of cuisines across the world, especially in Europe, they add over $3 billion per year to the world economy. Mussels are filter feeders, eating both phytoplankton and zooplankton using gills that stretch the entire length of their bodies and filter about 1 gallon (4 liters) of seawater an hour. Mussel beds greatly benefit the water quality in coastal areas.

Mussels act as a record of what's in the water, so they can be used to study our impacts on the oceans. Scientists have sampled mussel beds to map the presence of pollutants, including mercury, cadmium, lead, arsenic, plastic, and even cigarette butts. The filters of cigarettes clog the mussels, decreasing their filtration rates to one-third of normal levels.

24 *Atlantic Pearl Oyster*

PINCTADA IMBRICATA

CLASS
Bivalvia

RANGE
Subtropical Indo-Pacific
and Mediterranean

HABITAT
Rocky shoreline to depths
of 82 feet (25 m)

SIZE
Up to 4 inches (10 cm)

OF NOTE
Produces pearls

DISCOVER MORE

Confusingly, the Atlantic pearl oyster isn't found in the Atlantic, but rather in the Indo-Pacific, where it is native, and the Mediterranean, where it arrived five years after the opening of the Suez Canal. Sometimes it's also called the Gulf pearl oyster.

While this animal is the most widely distributed pearl oyster, others are also famous. The black-lipped oyster, *Pinctada margaritifera*, is prized for producing the highest-quality pearls. The largest pearl oyster *Pinctada maximus* grows up to 12 inches (30 cm) and is widely cultivated to produce what are known as South Sea pearls.

While any mollusk can technically make pearls, those made by most species lack the iridescence that makes them so prized by collectors. In the ocean, pearl oysters belong to the family Pteridae (meaning winged), owing to their shells with their fan-shaped rays. Freshwater mussels in the family Margaritiferidae are also famous for making pearls. That name comes from an old Persian word for pearl, and it is also the root of the name Margaret. The word pearl itself comes from the French word *perna*, which unexpectedly means leg. It's thought to reflect the thigh-like shape of many bivalves.

Ancient pearl hunters were recorded in writings from Sri Lanka, and confirmed by Pliny the Elder, especially in the Persian Gulf. Chinese pearl diving was also recorded during the Han dynasty in the South China Sea. Today, akoya pearls from Japan, as well as pearls from the South Sea and Tahiti, are among the most well known in the world of pearl farming, or periculture.

Pearls form when a small piece of debris gets caught up inside the oyster's shell. Despite the commonly held belief, the inciting irritant is very rarely a grain of sand, but more commonly a parasite or a piece of organic matter. Today's cultured pearls rely on a technique invented by British biologist William Saville-Kent. A small sphere, usually made from a freshwater mussel shell, is surgically inserted inside the pearl oyster's mantle.

The animal forms a sack around the irritant and deposits layers of the mineral aragonite and the horn-like protein conchiolin, which together form nacre, or mother-of-pearl, in the sac. This process is repeated over and over again. The luster of the pearl depends on how light passes through the layers of nacre. Thinner and more numerous layers are better at breaking up the light and enhance the reflective sheen. In its very structure, every pearl differs from other gems: it contains a trace of the struggle that made it beautiful.

25 *Ocean Quahog*

ARCTICA ISLANDICA

CLASS
Bivalvia

RANGE
North Carolina to Arctic

HABITAT
Sandy or mud seafloor
from 82 feet (25 m) to
1,310 feet (400 m)

SIZE
Up to 4½ inches (11 cm)

OF NOTE
The oldest animal
in the world

DISCOVER MORE

In 2006, scientists from Bangor University in Wales were working off the coast of Iceland studying clams, whose shells contain a record of seawater conditions in our warming oceans. The researchers dropped a trawl to the seafloor and pulled up about 200 ocean quahogs, one of which wasn't particularly big but looked especially old. They began to count the growth rings along the bivalve's hinge, which are laid down each year like rings on a tree trunk.

Ocean quahogs can live a long time— the researchers frequently found clams that topped a century. But the researchers passed 100 rings on this one, and then 200. They eventually reached 507. That ocean quahog remains the oldest individual animal ever discovered. (The record excludes colonial animals like corals, which can live more than a thousand years.)

Ocean quahogs (pronounced kwō hogs) are classically clam-shaped, with a thick, oval-shaped shell. They are black or brown on the outside with a cream-colored interior turning purple at the edges. The word quahog is thought to come from "popquauhock," which was the word for clam used by the Narragansett people who lived in what is today Rhode Island.

The clam is also called mahogany clam, black quahog, black clam, and Icelandic cyprine. The ocean quahog differs from the northern quahog (*Mercenaria mercenaria*), often found on New England beaches and popular on menus. It lives much deeper on the seafloor and is harvested with trawls. These bivalves are fished sustainably, and their populations remain at healthy levels.

The ancient clam pulled from the depths in Iceland was named Ming because, the researchers reasoned, it had been born a wee trochophore larva back in 1499, during that Chinese dynasty. The swath of human history the bivalve had lived through was breathtaking.

Later, in acknowledgment of its long life in North Atlantic waters, the ocean quahog was renamed for an Icelandic woman, Hafrún, meaning "mystery of the ocean." One of the mysteries Hafrún represents, though, has since been partly solved. In 2012, scientists discovered that ocean quahogs have an extraordinarily slow metabolism, allowing them to survive buried in sediments with almost no oxygen. This "life in the slow lane," they explained, is the key to their remarkable longevity. And while Hafrún's record-breaking age remains astonishing, researchers suspect even older quahogs still lie hidden deep on the ocean's floor.

26

Pilgrim's Scallop

PECTEN JACOBAEUS

CLASS
Bivalvia

RANGE
Mediterranean and Atlantic

HABITAT
Sand or mud seafloor
from 82 feet (25 m) to
660 feet (200 m)

SIZE
Up to 5½ inches (14 cm)

OF NOTE
Icon of pilgrims on the
Camino de Santiago

DISCOVER MORE

If you walk along the Camino de Santiago, which is a collection of many pilgrimage paths that run through the Iberian Peninsula and coalesce in northwestern Spain, you will see scallop shells dangling from a red string on the back of people's packs. Many are painted with the red sword of Saint James, who is buried in the cathedral in Santiago de Campostella at the pilgrimage's end. The scallop shell, whose radiating ribs similarly coalesce at one point, not only mirrors the trail map but was traditionally collected by travelers upon reaching the ocean as a symbol that they'd completed their trek. The shell was also useful as a cup or a bowl on their long walk home.

Only the lower of the animal's two shells would work as a vessel, however, as it is convex and usually whitish. The upper shell, which is flat and colored brown, orange, purple, or reddish, would work better as a lid. Each shell has fourteen to sixteen radiating rays with nearly rectangular "ears" alongside its hinge. The inside of the pilgrim's scallop shell is pearly white, like ceramic.

On the seafloor, a pilgrim's scallop peeks out from between its two shells with an array of short, beige tentacles and up to sixty pinhead-sized, blue eyes. Like all scallops, it can jet by quickly closing its shells, swimming several meters away from any perceived danger. The scallops filter seawater through their gills, sieving out the plankton on which they feed.

The range of the pilgrim's scallop is largely confined to the Mediterranean Sea, so it's possible that pilgrims who collected their scallop at one end of the Camino de Santiago might have gathered a different species, the great scallop (*Pecten maximus*), which lives in the Atlantic. You can tell them apart by looking at the edges of their shells: the pilgrim's scallop has squared-off edges, while the great scallop's edge is curvier. However, the difference may not be all that great after all, as the two types of scallops' ranges do overlap. Interbreeding is possible and scientists debate whether the two are actually the same species.

It's curious that the scientific name of the pilgrim's scallop is *Pecten jacobaeus,* rather than a name reflective of Saint James. That's because as James moves through languages it is modified to the Spanish Jaime, Italian Giacomo, Latin Jacobus, Greek Jacobos, and eventually Hebrew Jacob. Another way to view the chain of names is as a reminder that the reason a pilgrim sets off on a journey is also for transformation.

27

Noble Pen Shell

PINNA NOBILIS

CLASS
Bivalvia

RANGE
Mediterranean

HABITAT
Sand or mud seafloor
to depths of 196 feet (60 m)

SIZE
Up to 4 feet (1.2 m)

OF NOTE
Source of sea silk

DISCOVER MORE

Also known as the fan mussel, this bivalve is the largest in the Mediterranean, growing to a jaw-dropping 4 feet (1.2 m). The outside of the shell is striated and gray, sometimes stained with orange, and the inside is a brilliant mother-of-pearl.

The large space inside the noble pen shell hasn't gone unnoticed by a cadre of small crustaceans that like to make it their home. A pair of rust-colored shrimp (*Pontonia pinnophylax*) and a small, roundish pea crab (*Nepinnotheres pinnotheres*) are known to live inside the mussel. It's thought the consortium is a mutualistic one, meaning the animals help each other. The shrimp keeps an eye out for danger and gives the mussel a pinch when a predator approaches, so it knows to slam shut. The crustaceans feed on the mussel's food remains or waste products, keeping their bivalve host clean and tidy.

This mussel orients itself vertically, with its curved edge facing upward. Like all mussels, it makes byssus—long, sturdy threads that act like guide wires, keeping the animal fixed in place. The noble pen shell's byssal threads can reach more than 6 inches (15 cm) and have been prized for centuries as the source of sea silk.

The material made from this mollusk's byssus is said to be dainty and warm, shining like gold in the sunlight. One such fragment of sea silk was discovered in a woman's grave in Budapest in 1912, dated to the fourth century CE. Today, only a few women in Italy know how to collect, comb, spin, process, and weave sea silk, in part because these mollusks are critically endangered.

The noble pen shell is sensitive to pollution, so populations fell with industrialization, loss of the seagrass habitat, damage from boat anchoring, and ocean warming. The problems compounded in 2016, when Spanish researchers discovered that noble pen shell populations were undergoing a mass mortality. The culprit was traced to a newly identified protozoan parasite, and the epidemic spread unabated eastward across the Mediterranean. Only about ten locations remain where populations are still unaffected, in spots where salinity tends to be highly variable—conditions that the pathogen, perhaps, cannot withstand. The remaining resilient populations are monitored closely in the hope that one day these noble mollusks can be restored throughout the Mediterranean.

28

Tiger Cowrie

CYPRAEA TIGRIS

CLASS
Gastropoda

RANGE
Indian and Pacific

HABITAT
Coral reefs to depths of
131 feet (40 m)

SIZE
Up to 6 inches (15 cm)

OF NOTE
Hawaiian tiger cowrie
controls invasive sponges

DISCOVER MORE

Egg-shaped and very glossy, a young tiger cowrie has a tiger-striped shell that becomes dotted as the animal ages. The pattern of each shell is unique and in some places the dots can look bluish, or a reddish stripe might run down the upper surface. The underside of the shell is whitish in color, with a long, thin aperture lined with teeth. The juveniles eat algae, but the adults eat coral, sponges, and other invertebrates.

When a tiger cowrie is out hunting on the coral reefs of the Indian and Pacific oceans, its fleshy mantle flips up and over its shell. The underside has many small extrusions called papillae, which are used to sense chemicals and currents and possibly act as camouflage. When there's danger, the snail retracts inside its shell, keeping its tissue safe. This constant motion of the mantle across the shell's surface acts like a polisher, giving the shell its shine.

The tiger cowrie was first described by Swedish physician-turned-nature-namer, Carl Linnaeus, in his 1758 masterwork *Systema Naturae*, and the animal still bears the name he dubbed it. One wonders why he chose the species name *tigris* for the juvenile stripes rather than something based on a leopard, cheetah, or even a Dalmatian dog, which is more representative of the adult. Perhaps he wanted to emphasize that this is a tiger that changes its stripes.

The genus name *Cypraea* refers to the island of Cyprus, birthplace of Aphrodite, the goddess of femininity and fertility. Because of their rounded shape—similar to a woman's pregnant belly or an egg—cowries have been associated with fertility around the globe and are seen as amulets during pregnancy. In Japan, cowries, sometimes called *kaigara*, were held or placed near women in labor to encourage an easy delivery and to invoke the protective power of the sea.

Today's tiger cowrie includes at least four subspecies, which used to be considered separate. The most northeastern of these is also the largest, reaching 6 inches (15 cm) in length and living somewhat deeper than the others. It resides in Hawaiian waters, where it is known as *leho-kiko*. Hawaiian reefs have been invaded by at least ten non-indigenous sponge species, some of which are now more abundant than native sponges and compete for space with reef-building corals. Researchers discovered that the native tiger cowrie is a voracious predator of these invasive sponges, yet another of this gastropod's protective capabilities.

Glory-of-the-sea Cone

29

CONUS GLORIAMARIS

CLASS
Gastropoda

RANGE
Indo-Pacific

HABITAT
Coral reefs to depths of
984 feet (300 m)

SIZE
Up to 6 inches (15 cm)

OF NOTE
Once the world's most
expensive shell

DISCOVER MORE

There's a tale told about *Conus gloriamaris* that is set around the eighteenth century, a time when the glory-of-the-sea cone shell was revered throughout Europe. Undeniably beautiful, it has an elegant, slender shape and chestnut-colored markings that look like delicate netting or hieroglyphics. Although collectors readily acknowledged that more beautiful shells existed, the glory-of-the-sea cone was prized as the most valuable in the world. That was because only a single specimen had ever been found.

One day, the story goes, a ship arrived in the Netherlands from the Pacific Ocean, holding a second specimen of the rarest of all shells. An auction was held, drawing bidders from far and wide, including the owner of the previously lone glory-of-the-sea cone. The price rose higher and higher, but the owner made the winning bid. Once in possession of the second shell, he immediately smashed it to pieces. He wanted to hold on to the glory of owning the only one.

There's another story, perhaps also apocryphal, that at one auction a specimen sold for three times the price of Vermeer's famous painting *Woman in Blue Reading a Letter*. For the next 300 years, only a few dozen specimens of this shell were known to exist, which assumed positions of prestige in museums, curiosity cabinets, and private collections.

Scuba diving was invented in the second half of the twentieth century and divers soon discovered *Conus gloriamaris*'s habitats. It turned out that these snails are frequently encountered on muddy seafloors around tropical Pacific islands. Today, we know the range extends from Samoa west through the Philippines and Indonesia. Like other cone snails, they are carnivorous, attacking other mollusks with a spear-like radula through which they inject a mixture of potent toxins to subdue their prey.

Although collectors no longer prize the shell for its extreme rarity, and prices have fallen to just a couple of hundred dollars today, it's still valued for its beauty and fabled history.

30

Imperial Volute

CYMBIOLA IMPERIALIS

CLASS
Gastropoda

RANGE
Pacific

HABITAT
Sand or mud seafloor to
depths of 262 feet (80 m)

SIZE
Up to 10 inches (25 cm)

OF NOTE
It sports a sturdy crown
around its shoulders

DISCOVER MORE

Swedish physician and naturalist Carl
Linnaeus used the term "volute" in his
1758 masterwork *Systema Naturae* in
reference to the scroll-like shape at
the top of Ionic columns, which looks
a lot like the shells of this group of
carnivorous snails. He described them
in a few terse words of Latin: "*VOLUTA.*

*Animal Limax. Testa unilocularis, spiralis.
Apertura eîula, ecaudata, bafi emarginata.
Columella plicata: Labio interiore aut
umbilico nullo.*" Roughly translated, this
means slug-like animal with a single
spiral shell. The opening of the shell
has a spot for the siphon, the central
column is pleated, and there's no
flange on the lip.

Pleating on the central column is a characteristic feature of this group. No one knows exactly what its purpose is, but two ideas have been proposed. One is that it narrows the opening, making it harder for a predator to force its way inside. The other is that it acts like threads on a screw, aligning the tissue of the animal as it pulls itself inside, making retreat easier.

Although Linnaeus described more than two dozen species of volutes, the imperial volute was not among them. That attribution belongs to another naturalist, John Lightfoot (1735–88). Lightfoot named the animal *Voluta imperialis*, the imperial volute, for the rich crown of thick spines that surrounds the apex, which looks unmistakably like a king's crown. As taxonomic relationships were teased apart over the centuries, the genus name was changed to *Cymbiola*, meaning boat-shaped.

During the course of his life in science, Lightfoot became the curator of a large curiosity cabinet held by Margaret Bentinck, Duchess of Portland. Upon her death, he published a nearly 200-page catalog of her collection to be sold at auction in the spring of 1786. Item 4041 was described as "A magnificent specimen of *Voluta imperialis*, the most perfect one known, from the straits of Malacca [in today's Indonesia]—extremely scarce."

That imperial volute was the last of all the shells, corals, and minerals put on the auction block, perhaps an indication of the great value Lightfoot placed on the shell. It's hard not to wonder what the cleric might have felt watching the "most perfect one known" pass into the possession of someone else.

Further Reading

BOOKS

Abbott, R. Tucker and S. Peter Dance, *Compendium of Seashells: A Full-Color Guide to More than 4,200 of the World's Marine Shells* (1982) EP Dutton, New York, 421 pages

Abbott, R. Tucker, *Seashells of the World* (2001) Golden Guides from St. Martin's Press, New York, 160 pages

Allison, Sandy, *Seashells of New England: A Beachcombers Guide* (2017) Globe Pequot, Cuilford, Connecticut, 121 pages

Barnett, Cynthia, *The Sound of the Sea: Seashells and the Fate of the Oceans* (2021) W.W. Norton, New York, 432 pages

Cutler, Alan, *The Seashell on the Mountaintop: A Story of Science Sainthood and the Humble Genius Who Discovered a New History of the Earth* (2003) Dutton, New York, 240 pages

Dance, S. Peter, *Smithsonian Handbooks: Shells* (1992, 2022) DK London, 256 pages

Haeckel, Ernst, *Kunstformen der Natur.* (1904) Verlag des Bibliographischen Instituts, Leipzig and Vienna, 548 pages

Lindberg, Anne Morrow, *Gift from the Sea* (1955, 1975) Pantheon Books, New York, 138 pages

North Carolina Sea Grant (edited by Katie Mosher), *Seashells of North Carolina* (2024) University of North Carolina Press, 237 pages

Romashko, Sandra, *The Complete Collectors Guide to Shells and Shelling* (2004) Windward Publishing, Minneapolis, Minnesota, 128 pages

Scales, Helen, *Spirals in Time: The Secret Life and Curious Afterlife of Seashells* (2016) Bloomsbury Sigma, London, 304 pages

Staaf, Danna, *The Lady and the Octopus: How Jeanne Villepreux-Power Invented Aquariums and Revolutionized Marine Biology*, (2022) Carolrhoda Books, Minneapolis, Minnesota, 136 pages

Tunnell, John W. Jr., Barrera, Noe C., and Moretzohn, Fabio, *Texas Seashells: A Field Guide* (2014) Texas A&M University Press, 278 pages

Witherington, Blair and Dawn, *Florida's Seashells: A Beachcomber's Guide* (2017) Pineapple Press, Palm Beach, Florida, 88 pages

Yonge, C. Maurice, *The Sea Shore* (1949, 1971) Collins, London, 311 pages

ARTICLES

Barber A.H., Lu D., Pugno N.M., *Extreme strength observed in limpet teeth* (2015), Journal of the Royal Society

Callier, Viviane, *What Scallops' Many Eyes Can Teach Us About the Evolution of Vision* (2019), Smithsonian Magazine

Cronin, Dana, *California's Beloved Abalone Sea Snails Are Struggling. Here's Why* (2024), KQED

Elliot, Danielle, *Ming the clam, world's oldest animal, was actually 507 years old* (2013), CBS News

Holmes, Oliver Wendell, *The Chambered Nautilus* (1858), Originally published in *The Atlantic Monthly*

Langlois, Krista, *The Symbolic Seashell*, (2019), Hakai Magazine

Shefchik, Claire, *There's a Massive Conch-Shell Graveyard in the Caribbean* (2019), Atlas Obscura

Stein, Eliot, *The last surviving sea silk seamstress* (2017), BBC

Thomas, Elin et al., *A Global Red List for Hydrothermal Vent Molluscs* (2021), Frontiers in Marine Science

Tunnell, Jace, *Lightning whelks: The official state shell of Texas is also a fascinating marine predator* (2025), Caller Times

Watson, Parker and Sheri Shuck-Hall, *Oyster Harvesting in the Chesapeake Bay, Then and Now* (2023), Explore History, Christopher Newport University

ONLINE RESOURCES

The American Malacological Society
https://ams.wildapricot.org/

Bailey-Matthews National Shell Museum & Aquarium,
https://shellmuseum.org/shells-and-science

Beachcombing Magazine
https://www.beachcombingmagazine.com/

Conchologists of America
https://conchologistsofamerica.org/

Hardy's Internet Guide to Marine Gastropods *https://conchology.be/*

Journal of Molluscan Studies
https://academic.oup.com/mollus

Malacologia: International Journal of Malacology
https://instituteofmalacology.org/

The Malacological Society of London
https://malacsoc.org.uk/

Glossary

Adductor: bivalve muscle that pulls shut its two shells.

Ammonites: extinct cephalopods with chambered shells found as fossils.

Aperture: opening of gastropod, tusk, and nautilus shells.

Apex: oldest part of a gastropod shell, usually pointed.

Aplacophora: deep-water mollusks without shells.

Axis: line from apex to umbilicus of a gastropod shell.

Belemnites: extinct cephalopods with internal shells found as dart-like fossils.

Bivalve: diverse class of mollusks with two hinged shells.

Bioluminescence: light production by a living organism.

Byssus/byssal threads: strong, hair-like strands secreted by some bivalves, used to secure the animal to a surface.

Cephalopods: swimming mollusks characterized by a head surrounded by many flexible arms.

Chitinous: made from a tough, flexible protein called chiton.

Chiton: marine mollusk with eight overlapping calcareous plates, class Polyplacophora, that lives on rocks.

Coccolithophores: single-celled phytoplankton that grow intricate, plate-like calcium carbonate tests.

Conchiolin: group of proteins forming the organic part of mollusk shells.

Conchologist: one who studies mollusk shells.

Conchomancy: use of shells to predict the future or gain insight.

Conical: cone-shaped gastropod shell whose width and height are roughly equal.

Conotoxin: neurologically active toxin in cone snail venom.

Crinoid: sea lily or feather star echinoderm, frequently found as fossils.

Costae: pronounced ribbing that continues across gastropod whorls, characteristic of a wentletrap.

Depressed: gastropod shell whose width is greater than its height.

Dextral: typical spin of a gastropod shell; clockwise viewed from apex.

Diatom: single-celled zooplankton that secrete ornate, glass-like tests.

Egg case: protective capsule containing the eggs of some mollusks.

Filter feeding: sieving seawater for small food such as plankton.

Foraminifera: single-celled zooplankton that secrete ornate calcium carbonate tests.

Gastropod: most diverse class of mollusks, characterized by having a single shell if present; includes snails and slugs.

Globose: a rounded gastropod shell whose width and height are roughly equal.

Ligament: in bivalves, an elastic, multilayered structure joining the two valves.

Lip: outer edge of a gastropod shell.

Malacology: the study of mollusks.

Mantle: outer tissue layer of a mollusk that secretes the shell.

Micromollusk: mollusk whose shell is roughly smaller than ¼ inch (6 mm).

Mollusk: very diverse phylum of animals with a soft, unsegmented body, a mantle, and often a protective calcareous shell.

Monoplacophora: deep-sea mollusks resembling limpets, but whose anatomy is quite different.

Nacre/nacreous: iridescent inner shell layer of some mollusks, also called mother of pearl.

Neuston: animals that live at the ocean/air surface.

Oblong: gastropod shell whose height is greater than its width.

Ocelli (singular: ocellus): light-sensitive cells that act as simple eyes, also called eyespots.

Operculum: horny or calcareous plate on a gastropod's foot used as a door to the aperture.

Orthoceras: extinct cephalopods with a long, chambered, conical shell.

Periostracum: horny, chitinous outer layer of mollusk shells.

Photophore: organ that emits bioluminescence.

Phytoplankton: single-celled plankton that perform photosynthesis.

Plankton: diverse community of organisms that float in the ocean.

Protoconch: oldest part of gastropod or cephalopod shell.

Radiolarian: single-celled plankton with silicious shell and needle-like extensions.

Radula: flexible, tongue-like structure in most mollusks, but not bivalves; may have rows of horny teeth for scraping or cutting or be modified into a spear for stabbing.

Rib: gastropod shell ornament running in same direction as axis.

Sessile: living attached to a surface and unable to move.

Shoulder: pronounced ridge in a gastropod shell, marking a change in the shell's profile.

Sinistral: atypical spin of a gastropod shell; counterclockwise when viewed from apex.

Siphon: tube-like structure mollusks use for breathing, feeding, and locomotion.

Siphonal canal: trough- or notch-like extension of a gastropod shell's aperture where the siphon protrudes.

Spat: young scallop competent enough to settle out of the plankton.

Spire: top section of a gastropod shell, between the apex and the biggest whorl.

Suture: joints where whorls on a gastropod shell join.

Test: shell of an echinoderm, diatom, foraminiferan, or other protozoan plankton.

Trochophore: free-swimming, ciliated larva of a worm or mollusk.

Tusk shell: marine mollusks of the class Scaphopoda; look like elephant tusks

Umbo (plural: umbones): oldest part of a bivalve shell.

Umbilicus: hollow tube along a gastropod shell's axis around which the whorls coil.

Valve: one of a bivalve's two calcareous shells.

Veliger: gastropod or bivalve larva with ciliated membranes for swimming.

Whorl: complete 360-degree coil of a gastropod shell.

Zooplankton: protozoa, crustaceans, jellyfish, mollusks, worms, larvae, eggs etc. that float in the ocean.

GLOSSARY

Index

Index

Credits

Author Credits

I extend my gratitude to UniPress for the gift of being able to immerse myself in the incredible world of mollusks while writing this book. I've loved every minute of exploring their seas and discovering the many ways they've changed our lives. Special thanks to Claire Collins for the invitation, to Ruth Patrick for being a steady-handed delight, and to Alison Stevens for good-natured doggedness in the image archives. Also, thanks to Mylène Mozas-Sauvignon for making this book so gorgeous and to Lucy Vallance for wise editorial guidance. Appreciation beyond measure goes to my dad, David Berwald, for teaching me how to be a seeker in the natural world. Just as a mollusk owes its life to the support and protection of its shell, my biggest thanks go to those that surround me in laughter, joy, and security: Keith, Ben, and Isy, and of course, Blue and River.

Picture Credits

Alamy Stock Photo/Album: 47, 59, 81; Encyclopaedia Britannica: 101; Florilegius: 69; Mouseion Archives: 41; Penta Springs Limited: 130; The Picture Art Collection: 65 (right), 148, 149; Science History Images: 93

iStockphoto.com/The Nature Notes: 27, 90–91; THEPALMER: 29; ZU_09: 49, 84–85, 166

Shutterstock/arxichtu4ki: 4, 25